THE HANDBOOK OF

DREAMS

THE HANDBOOK OF
DREAMS

Sweet dreams...
and how to interpret them

JUDITH MILLIDGE

Published by SILVERDALE BOOKS
An imprint of Bookmart Ltd
Registered number 2372865
Trading as Bookmart Ltd
Desford Road
Enderby
Leicester LE19 4AD

© 2003 D&S Books Ltd

D&S Books Ltd
Kerswell,
Parkham Ash, Bideford
Devon, England
EX39 5PR

e-mail us at:-
enquiries@dsbooks.fsnet.co.uk

This edition printed 2003

ISBN 1-85605-770-4

Creative Director: Sarah King
Editor: Clare Haworth-Maden
Project editor: Yvonne Worth
Designer: 2H Design

Printed in China

1 3 5 7 9 10 8 6 4 2

CONTENTS

INTRODUCTION

'A readily reversible state of reduced awareness and metabolic activity that occurs periodically in many animals. Usually accompanied by physical relaxation, the onset of sleep in humans and other mammals is marked by a change in the electrical activity of the brain. . .'

Oxford Reference Concise Science Dictionary

We spend over a third of our lives asleep and, according to scientists, enjoy between three and six dreams a night. Dreaming is a universal human activity, over which we have little control, and, until recently, very little concrete knowledge. Scientists have analysed physical changes in our sleep patterns, but no one can state with any certainty why we dream or whether our dreams have any real significance. Dreams are intensely personal experiences, known only to the dreamer unless they choose to share it with someone. They are visual experiences and, often, mere words are not

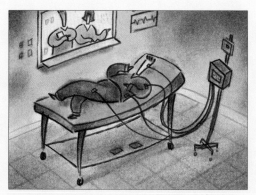

'Sleep laboratories' have been established in a number of universities and research institutes and exist to study both the effects of sleep on the human body as well as the purpose of dreams. Doctors use them primarily to assess and cure sleep disorders such as narcolepsy, sleep apnoea and insomnia, while psychologists can assess the effects of sleep or sleep deprivation on the brain. Patients are tucked up in bed with electrodes attached to their scalp which enable the sleep technicians to measure the brain's electrical activity during sleep. Once dismissed as fringe medicine, sleep laboratories have gained academic respectability throughout the world.

enough to convey the subtle nuances involved. Furthermore, we all have unique dreams woven from the threads of our conscious lives, our hopes, fears, memories and imagination. Should we pay attention to what appear to be the messages within them, or are they just the bizarre working of a brain trying to sort the events of daily life into some sort of order?

By and large, dreams are associated with pleasure and relaxation; the restorative properties of sleep and dreams feature in literature, music and art throughout the world. People seem infatuated by the sheer entertainment value of their dreams, surprised that such colourful and bizarre images could emerge from minds that, by day, are confined to the mundane or repetitive. And it is this simple fact that forms the basis of our fascination with our dreams: surely such mesmerising, often illogical and engaging, images and stories must mean something?

Dreams and dreaming usually raise more questions than solutions, however – the first being the perennial cry of frustration, 'Why can't I remember my dreams?' The second, prompted by tantalising glimpses of brilliance and half-remembered shafts of pleasure, is to wonder

how and why one's brain has managed to conjure up tales worthy of a Hollywood movie. And the third is what does it all mean?

The power to interpret dreams has occupied the great and the good in every generation for centuries. In the distant past, plausible interpreters could make themselves powerful and invaluable to princes and rulers, and today, there is a plethora of books, magazines and websites devoted to understanding dreams. But before we can embark on the quest to understand our dreams, we must first examine the 'stuff of which dreams are made': sleep.

To sleep!
Perchance to dream...

Young children often have very vivid dreams which they have trouble separating from reality.

Human beings need sleep to restore their bodies physically after the rigours of the day. The metabolism slows down, the immune system can focus on fighting infections and we awake refreshed after eight hours or so of sleep. Without this vital chance to rest, mental function is severely impaired, people actually look exhausted and hard physical activity becomes extremely difficult. Having said that, sleep deprivation does not produce any actual physical illness. People need different amounts of sleep, and sleep requirements vary according to age. Babies sleep for 15 hours a day, most adults require between five and eight hours a night, whereas older individuals may sleep for shorter periods.

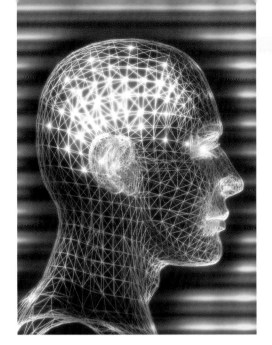

EEG readings show that electrical activity in the brain alters radically as we sleep.

It is now thought that dreams might play an important role in allowing the human brain to rest and recuperate. With the body operating on autopilot while we sleep, brain activity is limited to maintaining the functions vital to life – primarily respiratory and cardiac functions. One theory is that dreams are merely the means by which the brain maintains a level of alertness and stimulation necessary to survive: the brain's answer to an entertaining video, watched while we relax. Without the outlet of these electrical impulses of the imagination, the brain might simply shut down. If this is true, dreams are critical to human survival.

Rapid Eye Movement (REM) sleep was first identified in 1955 by the scientists Eugene Aserinsky and Nathaniel Kleitmen who noted that, at certain points during a period of shallow sleep, the eyelids began to move as though the eyes were darting around following activities or moving figures. They also discovered that during REM, the flow of blood to the brain increased, breathing and heartbeat were sometimes irregular and there was a reduction in electrical activity in some muscles. They revealed that a person woken during REM sleep could recount dramatic dreams, whereas only six per cent of non-REM sleepers

Older people generally need less sleep, and often cat-nap during the day.

Sleep requirements vary between individuals and range from between about five and nine hours for healthy adults. British Prime Minister Margaret Thatcher famously thrived on only three or four hours per night, while President Ronald Reagan, her counterpart in the White House during much of the 1980s, needed not only the full eight hours, but apparently the odd nap as well in order to run the country. While a lack of sleep affects moods and physical and mental functioning during the day, it does not cause any actual physical illness and the human body is remarkably adept at replenishing lost sleep. In one famous experiment, a man deprived of sleep for over 200 hours, who had experienced paranoia and hallucinations in the latter stages, felt refreshed and restored after just one night of nine hours sleep.

thought they had been dreaming. Aserinsky and Kleitman used an electroencephalograph (EEG) machine to monitor the brain's electrical activity; the readings showed spiky alpha waves during wakefulness which changed to slower regular theta waves as the sleeper drifted into sleep.

Scientists who study the mechanics of sleep divide it into four stages, based on the measurement of electrical brain activity; brain waves become deeper and slower the more deeply we sleep. The finer line between waking and sleeping is known as the 'hypnogogic' state. This is the point at which the muscles relax, the eyeballs roll back and the sleeper may feel as though they are floating. They may begin to dream as images float in front of them, although EEG readings show that the mind is still active.

As the EEG waves change to rounded theta waves, the sleeper enters 'stage one' sleep, which lasts about ten minutes. The EEG patterns change again to produce 'spindle' waves and large, steep waves known as 'K-complexes' which indicate the rapid brain activity of 'stage two' sleep. Although the sleeper is definitely asleep, if woken they may deny that they have been sleeping. After 15 to 30 minutes, large delta waves mark the progression to the deeper 'stage three' and 'stage four' sleep.

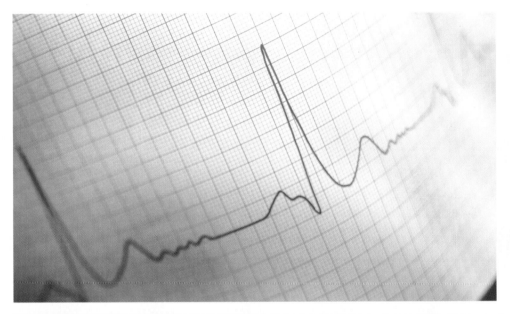

It was not until the 1950s that scientists could study the physiological effects of sleep on the human body. Until that time, any conclusions about sleep and dreams were largely based on guess-work and hypotheses. The EEG, or electroencephalograph, uses sensors attached to a sleeper's scalp to measure the electrical activity of the brain and is primarily used in medicine to assess brain damage. However, it is also immensely valuable in studying the brain's activity during sleep. The 'brain waves' generated by tiny electrical impulses that dart across the synapses of the brain vary immensely during different phases of sleep and interestingly the period of REM sleep when we dream produces the most activity.

About 90 minutes after falling asleep, the brain waves revert to the spindles and K-complexes of stage two sleep and the brain enters a ten-minute phase of REM sleep – the period when we dream. After that, sleepers travel through the sleep cycle in reverse, the whole process lasting about 90 minutes. During eight hours, most people average four sleep cycles, with each period of REM sleep getting progressively longer, until the last extends to as long as an hour.

Non-REM sleep, when the mind is unconscious, seems to be the time when the physical body rests. This period of deep sleep is when sleepers may walk or talk; during REM sleep, the limbs are paralysed, a safety measure which prevents sleepers from engaging in whatever activity is occurring in the dream world. Physiological activity, however, is often immense. During REM sleep, blood flow through the brain increases by 40 per cent compared to

In an attempt to gain a deeper understanding of human sleep requirements and the importance or otherwise of dreams, sleep researchers have studied the sleep patterns of other mammals and of babies in the womb. Most animals and birds spend some time asleep, although the length of their daily rest varies greatly. Some animals sleep at times when they are most vulnerable to predators, retreating to warrens, trees or burrows out of danger. Mammalian sleep patterns vary dramatically and the differences are governed partly by whether an animal is a predator or prey. Big cats such as lions and tigers can afford to spend 70 per cent of their time snoozing, while prey species sleep fitfully for much shorter periods.

Dogs sleep for between ten and 13 hours a day, depending largely on the breed and the extent of their physical activity. They wake up more frequently than humans and just like humans, they experience REM sleep, which takes up about 25 per cent of their sleep time. Each burst of REM sleep lasts approximately five minutes. Owners often note that their pets roll, bark and growl as they dream of chasing cats or rabbits, or simply of digging up an enormous bone.

Dolphins, like most sea mammals, sleep near the surface so that its blowhole is just below the waves. Evolution has enabled dolphins to shut down half the brain at a time, with one half experiencing deep sleep for up to four hours, while the other half remains awake for protection and survival.

Interestingly, all mammals experience REM sleep, although this may not surprise the dog owners who have watched their sleeping pets yelp and wriggle while asleep. Dolphins sleep with only half of their brain shut down and one eye shut, the functioning half being sufficient to help it survive. Babies in the womb experience about ten hours of REM sleep in the month before birth, although this drops to about five hours when they are a year old. These figures may add weight to the theory that dreams are a necessary stimulation for the brain, designed to keep it active.

the flow during non-REM slumber. Breathing is often erratic, one minute panting as though from great exertion, the next, almost stilled, paused as though the dreamer were holding their breath. Blood pressure rises and falls dramatically, often reaching heights that would seriously worry the men in white coats during waking hours, and the kidneys produce more concentrated urine. So, with all this activity, it is hardly surprising that sleepers sometimes wake up feeling less than refreshed after a night's sleep!

Any woman in the advanced stages of pregnancy is aware that her foetus has periods of intense activity interspersed with periods of quiet. Babies *in utero* definitely experience REM sleep, but quite what their dreams consist of is a mystery. They have about ten hours of REM sleep every day, a tremendous

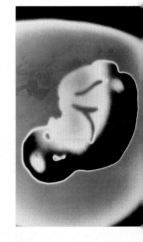

amount in comparison to later sleep patterns, which declines rapidly after birth when it falls to about five hours a day after a year.

Dreams
around the world

The Tibetan *Book of the Dead* calls dreaming an intermediate stage between life and death, and many Tibetans believe that sleep is a necessary preparation for the inevitable. Dreams are important in Tibetan culture and many people believe they are vital to their spiritual health and growth, so remembering dreams is an important skill to be learnt. One effective method of Tibetan dream recall is to imagine that there is a glowing blue sphere in your throat in which you place your desire to remember your dreams. Hold this powerful image in your mind as you fall asleep and with luck and practice, you will not forget your dreams on waking.

Many ancient cultures set great store by their dreams and use them to influence their daily activities. The ancient Chinese regarded dreams as the experiences of the soul, which went wandering while the body slept – rather like an out-of-body experience. The Taoist philosopher Chuang-Tzu encapsulated the feeling of being unable to differentiate between reality and the dream world one often experiences on waking:

'Once upon a time, I Chuang-Tzu dreamed I was a butterfly fluttering hither and thither, to all intents and purposes a butterfly. I was aware only of following my fancy as a butterfly and unconscious of my human individuality. Suddenly, I awoke and there I lay, myself again. Now I do not know whether I was then a man dreaming I was a butterfly or whether I am now a butterfly dreaming I am a man.'

Many Native American tribes believed in the power of dreams and established rituals such as the 'Honoraria' in which dreams were acted out before members of the tribe. They believed that if the messages of the dreams were not heeded, great misfortune would befall the tribe. Native Americans believed in the power of shamans to act as healers or diviners and interpreters of dreams. As part of their initiation they drew a magical circle around the dreamer and then incubated his dreams and visions. Dream catchers, like the one pictured are physical manifestations of theses magical circles and are intended to catch messages from the spirits of the elements and land.

In Tibet people frequently share their dreams with their companions, entertaining each other with the bizarre tales thrown out by their unconscious minds. They take their dreams quite seriously, and if troubled by a particularly memorable or stirring dream, they may visit the local monastery where there is usually a monk skilled in the art of dream interpretation. Interestingly, the Tibetans, who inhabit the high mountains of the Himalayas, claim that their dreams are more frequent and more intense when they are at high altitudes.

Some African societies believe that dreams are sent by their ancestors to warn and advise them. The Zulu people share their dreams with each other and refer to their tribal dream interpreter as 'head man'. Native American tribes encourage children to remember their dreams from an early age and use 'dream catchers' to trap the evil spirits that might harm the sleeper. Like the Zulu in Africa, Huron and Iroquois Indians shared their dreams and used them to formulate tribal policy.

Interpretations
of dreams

Many cultures have believed that dreams were sent by demons, or evil spirits.

From the earliest time of recorded history, people have believed that dreams were important. They were regarded as supernatural messages sent by the gods to direct or forewarn mankind. The ancient Babylonian *Epic of Gilgamesh*, inscribed on stone tablets 6,000 years before the birth of Christ, is the story of Gilgamesh, King of Uruk, a man troubled by vivid nightmares. The tale reflects the Babylonian obsession with dreams, and their belief that they were sent by demons and spirits. They had a fatalistic and pessimistic attitude towards them and built a temple to Mamu, goddess of dreams, in order to protect themselves from these malign spirits.

Like the Babylonians, the ancient Egyptians regarded dreams as warnings, but believed they came directly from the gods, rather than from spirits. They were the first civilisation to practise dream incubation – using dreams to ask the gods for guidance. Put to sleep in a temple dedicated to the god Imhotep, sleepers in search of healing had their dreams interpreted by the priest or 'Master of Secret Things'. There were many temples dedicated to Serapis, the god of dreams, the most famous being at Memphis dating from 3000 BC, although the earliest surviving account of dream interpretation in ancient Egypt dates from 1350 BC.

The tradition of dream incubation was continued by the ancient Greeks. They also regarded dreams as divine messages and sought intervention via Aesklepius, the god of healing. There were 300 temples devoted to Aesklepius scattered throughout Greece,

The Ancient Egyptians paid great attention to their dreams, and one of the earliest recorded dreams is that of the King Thotmes IV. It is engraved on a sheet of granite which rests between the paws of the Sphinx, the monument Thotmes vowed to maintain for the rest of his life.

The caduceus, a universal medical emblem, originated as the symbol of Aesklepius, the Greek god of healing.

the most famous at Epidaurus. All were places of great beauty, located in woods near to sacred streams or the sea. Patients were ritually purified before entering a snake-filled temple and being put to sleep under the influence of the god Hypnos (and a sleeping draught). Visited in their sleep by Aesklepius, the patients were apparently licked by sacred snakes and so cured of their troubles. No interpretation of their dream was necessary. It is this tradition that gave rise to the enduring medical symbol of two snakes entwined around a staff.

The Greek philosopher Heraclitus (c. 450–375 BC) was an early interpreter of dreams, and really the first to realise that dreams and their meanings were not only man-made rather than divinely inspired, but also pretty much unique to individuals: 'For the waking there is one common world only; but when asleep, each man turns to his own private world.' Hippocrates (the 'father of modern medicine' 460–377 BC) persisted in the idea that dreams stemmed from astrological or divine influences and also anticipated the work of Freud, in stating that symbols were important in dreams. He believed that dreams could be used to diagnose illness. A dream of a flood, for example, was a sign that the dreamer had too much blood and needed bleeding.

Aristotle (384–322 BC) took a far more lucid and, to modern minds, rational view of dreams, noting that, 'The most skillful interpreter of dreams is he who has the faculty of observing resemblances. Any one may interpret dreams which are vivid and plain.' Arguing that dreams could not be god-sent simply because animals also dreamed, he observed that the hallucinations of mental patients had much in common with ordinary dreams. He suggested that dreams were merely a kaleidoscope of the day's events, but also acknowledged that dreams contained symbols, which may refer to mundane aspects of the waking life. Plato (427–347 BC) realised that people dreamed of doing things they would be ashamed of doing in real life: 'The virtuous man is content to *dream* what a wicked man really *does*.'

The images and scenarios of our dreams are completely unpredictable. They may be based on the activities of the waking life, or they may contain surreal images unrelated to reality.

The first really comprehensive work of dream interpretation is Roman and dates from AD 150. The five-volume *Oneirocritica* or *Interpretation of Dreams* was the work of Artemidorus, a philosopher and soothsayer who travelled extensively throughout the Roman Empire amassing all the contemporary knowledge he could find about dreams. He believed that dreams were full of symbols and should rarely

Jung believed that everyone shares a common heritage of primordial imagery.

be taken at face value; he examined the recurrence of the same types of symbols in dreams across the world and the existence of certain fundamental dreams across cultures. Crucially, he acknowledged the importance of the individual's circumstance in attempting to elicit the meaning of a dream: 'The same dream does not always have the same meaning in each case and for each person... we need to take note of whether the person dreaming is male or female, healthy or sick, a free man or a slave, rich or poor, young or old.' Nearly two thousand years later, Freud acknowledged the importance of Artemidorus's work and, in a tribute to the Roman, gave his own great opus the same title.

It is probably safe to say that there was no further great revelatory work on dreams in Western civilisation until the 18th century. There followed a period packed with visionaries, theorists and great dreamers. The Renaissance saw an outpouring of dream dictionaries published to meet public demand, most of them based on the work of Artemidorus. It was not until the Enlightenment of the late 18th century

The Romans took great interest in dreams, although the most famous Roman of them all, Julius Caesar, ignored his wife's dream which warned him to 'Beware the ides of March'.

over time, with the early church fathers of the 4th century believing in the possibility of divinely inspired dreams. St Augustine (354–430) knew that his unconscious was the part of his functioning mind over which he had little or no control: 'I cannot grasp all that I am' he wrote, fearing that God would punish him for his worldly dreams. His near contemporary, the theologian Gregory of Nyassa (331–395) assumed that dreams occurred in sleep while the intellect was at rest. In his treatise, *On the Making of Man*, he noted that the dream mind, free of the normal restraining influence

The medieval Christian church disapproved of dream interpretation.

that thinkers began to question seriously the meaning of dreams once again.

One reason for the dearth of intellectual exploration was the tight grip of the Roman Catholic church on the conscience of western Europe. The attitude of Christian theologians altered of the intellect, is governed by 'man's brute nature' and so passions run wild, throwing up all sorts of images undreamed of during the waking hours.

By the Middle Ages, doctrine had altered substantially, with scholars such as St Thomas Aquinas (1225–74) stating that dreams could never be considered prophetic as the future was firmly under God's control; thus anyone claiming to have a vision or prophetic dream could only be a blasphemer. So Joan of Arc's visions about expelling the English from France in the 15th century, while touching a popular nerve and winning royal favour, attracted the ire of the church which extracted the ultimate penalty: condemnation as a witch and burning at the stake.

While dreams continued to fascinate a great many people, it was not until the end of the 18th century that essayists recognised that dreams were the products of the unconscious mind. In 1867 the physician of 'nervous disorders', Henry Maudsley noted that the sleeping mind was able to produce 'the most vivid dramas', but did not explore the possibilities of dreams any further.

The most renowned study of dreams emerged in 1899 from the pen of the Viennese psychologist Sigmund Freud (1856–1939) when he published *The Interpretation of Dreams*. Freud's work was groundbreaking for several

Women who claimed to be able to interpret dreams were often persecuted as witches.

Sigmund Freud is, without doubt, the father of modern dream interpretation. He was the first to address seriously the question of the importance of dreams to psychological well-being and to try to formulate an idea of what they mean. However, he was very much a man of his times and many of his theories reflect the traditional 'Victorian values' of his era.

prevalent at the end of the 19th century.

Freud used a new technique of 'free association' to help his patients interpret their dreams – and he was keen to stress that the dreamer's interpretation was more important than that of the analyst. He recognised that dreams were the products of the subconscious mind, which overrode the usual restrictions imposed by the conscience by the use of symbols. Thus Freud believed that 'the content of a dream is the representation of an unfulfilled wish'.

reasons, and all serious dream researchers still acknowledge the debt owed to him as the originator of psychoanalysis. He studied dreams to gain an insight into psychological problems in defiance of contemporary medical thinking, which largely ignored such issues. Furthermore, he addressed the question of sex, and although his insistence on finding sexual imagery in the most mundane objects has been largely discredited, his work helped remove some of the sexual repression

Dream interpretation entered a new dimension with the work of Carl Jung (1875–1961). Jung worked with Freud for several years, from 1907 until 1913, but it was clear by 1911 that Jung

A medical student, Carl Jung went on to work at the Burgholzli mental clinic and he met Freud in Vienna in 1907. He collaborated with Freud for several years, but as time went by, his theories diverged from those of his mentor. A year after the publication of *The Psychology of the Unconscious* in 1912, he split from Freud and developed his own school of analytical psychology.

Fire implies heat, danger, passion and protection. Fires can be a source of comfort and warmth, in their most basic form a means of survival in the wilderness, or a metaphor for human passion.

rejected Freud's emphasis on wish fulfilment. A keen anthropologist, Jung had studied comparative religion, examining the belief systems, mythology and symbols of cultures throughout the world. He was convinced that a number of key symbols or archetypes were common to civilisations centuries apart and separated by thousands of miles, and this study formed the basis of his theory of the collective unconscious. He believed that these primordial images were passed from generation to generation in the same way that physical characteristics are transmitted. Unlike Freud, who gave a fixed meaning to every image, Jung amplified the meaning of symbols by considering the dreamer's background and circumstances.

Jung's theories have been reinforced by the work of other anthropologists. For example, the second-century dream interpreter Artemidorus noted that a dream of fire in the sky heralded war or famine, while one African tribe in Malawi regarded bush fire as a sign that war was expected. Artemidorus interpreted a dream about losing a tooth as a sign that the dreamer would lose a member of his household; for the Africans it meant the death of a wife or child.

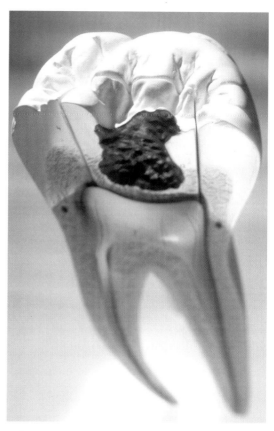

A dream about teeth may be related to fears about money, or perhaps about old age. A person without teeth is commonly regarded as powerless.

Dreams and religion

Dreams have an important significance in many of the world's great religions. In the Bible, Joseph's interpretation of Pharaoh's dream brought him prosperity and freedom and in the Book of Daniel, Nebuchadnezzar summoned Daniel, a dream interpreter, to explain his puzzling dream. The king had seen a tall abundant tree at the centre of the earth, surrounded by wild beasts and nesting birds. A messenger from

In the Bible, Joseph's ability to interpret Pharaoh's dream is what lead to his freedom and reunion with his family. Joseph's experience underlines the importance the ancient Egyptians attached to the interpretation of dreams.

Moslems believe that good dreams (*ruya*) are the gift of Allah to the faithful, while bad dreams (*hulm*) are sent by the devil to taunt them.

heaven had ordered the tree to be cut down and the king chained to the stump to live like an animal, grazing on grass. Daniel believed that the dream was a message to Nebuchadnezzar, warning that there was a power greater than his, and that in God's eyes he was no more important than a beast of the field.

Buddha's mother Queen Maya dreamed of the birth of her son and saw the future Buddha emerge from her womb in the form of a white elephant. Her dream was interpreted by 64 holy Brahmins who predicted her son would become either a world monarch or a world saviour.

In Deuteronomy a note of skepticism creeps in, when it states that a dreamer whose message encourages apostasy should be put to death. 'If prophet or those who divine by dreams appear among you... and say, "Let us follow other gods", ...you must not heed the words...' (Deut. 13). In the New Testament messages are conveyed from God in dreams: an angel appears in a dream to Joseph explaining that he should marry Mary, and in another dream an angel warns of Herod's impending massacre of the first born.

Moslems believe that the Prophet Mohammad founded Islam in AD 610 after a dream in which the Angel Gabriel took him first to Jerusalem, and then to heaven, where he met Adam, Christ and the four Evangelists. These revelations, which happened in Mecca, prompted the foundation of a great new faith, and Mohammad told his followers that good dreams were a sign of Allah's blessing, whereas bad dreams came from the devil.

The 'path to enlightenment' was received by Buddha in a dream, and Hindu tradition accords certain dream images great importance, linking them with the symbolic attributes of gods and demons. The ancient Hindu text, the *Atharva Veda* includes a passage on dream interpretation, noting that in a series of dreams, only the last one is significant.

In Hindu belief, the Vishnu is regarded as the divine dreamer of the world dream, and all of creation is part of that dream. He sleeps on the great serpent Ananta (meaning 'endless') and his dream is often depicted in art as a great lotus plant growing from his navel, with the dream unfolding like a beautiful flower.

Famous dreamers

Many creative people have used their dreams as the basis for their work, others have 'slept on' a problem to find that, on waking, that the answer has become clear. The poet Samuel Taylor Coleridge (1772–1834) famously dreamed the verses of *Kubla Khan, a Vision in a Dream* and was in the process of writing down the first of two hundred or so lines, when he was interrupted by 'a person on business from Porlock'. The interruption broke his concentration, and the rest of the poem 'passed away like the images on the surface of a stream'. Coleridge's poem is, nonetheless, a masterpiece of dream-like imagery (perhaps made all the more powerful by the dose of opium he had consumed before falling asleep):

'In Xanadu did Kubla Khan

A stately pleasure dome decree:

Where Alph the sacred river, ran

Through caverns measureless to man

Down to a sunless sea...'

The writer Graham Greene apparently used his dreams to help construct and plot his novels, the poet W B Yeats was often inspired by his dreams and Paul McCartney dreamed the tune of Yesterday. In 1819 Mary Shelley fell asleep quickly after discussing the supernatural with Lord Byron and Percy Bysshe Shelley but was disturbed by a powerful dream, which she committed to paper the next day. Frankenstein: or, The Modern Prometheus had scared her, and she believed that the story would terrify her readers.

Predictive dreams

There are certain classic dreams to which we are all prey at some time or another – dreams of falling, or of abandonment, for example. Anthropologists have distinguished four basic types of dream among ancient cultures: 'big' dreams, which have cultural significance; prophetic dreams, warning of the future; healing dreams that promote good health; and 'little' dreams of significance only to the dreamer. The question of whether or not precognitive dreams can predict the future is controversial, but there are countless anecdotal examples of people who claim to have seen their fate in a dream. Similarly, many rulers have tried to use their dreams to influence their actions and some were consequently in thrall to soothsayers or mystics who claimed to be able to interpret dreams. One rather poor example for this kind of enlightened governance is Adolf Hitler, who apparently made decisions based on the advice of his dream analyst.

Many people dream that they are lost in a crowd, perhaps that their very identity has disappeared.

A wise and pragmatic soul, President Abraham Lincoln was sorely shaken by his dream of his own death, which occurred only a few days before his assassination.

There are many instances of people who have dreamed of disasters, assassinations or personal tragedies before the events have happened. Others claim to have dreamed of disasters while they were happening, perhaps tuning in telepathically to the suffering of others thousands of miles away. In 1912 a New York woman dreamed that her mother was in a lifeboat so crowded it was on the verge of capsizing. When she told her husband about the dream, he pointed out that her mother was safe in Europe, but when the papers displayed the news of the sinking of the *Titanic* the next day, the mother's name was on the passenger list. She did in fact survive, and told her daughter of the dreadful experience of being crammed in a lifeboat and being so certain of death that she could think of nothing but her daughter.

US President Abraham Lincoln (1809–65) dreamt of his own death a few days before his assassination in 1865 and recounted the dream to a friend. 'There seemed to be a deathlike stillness about me. Before me was a catafalque on which rested a corpse wrapped in funeral vestments. "Who is dead in the White House", I demanded of one of the soldiers. "The President", was his answer; "he was killed by an assassin!" Then came a loud burst of grief from the crowd, which woke me from my dream. I slept no more that night; and although it was only a dream, I have been strangely troubled by it ever since.'

Many of us have nightmares about disasters wrecking our lives. Fortunately, most are simply dreams and do not come true.

Lucid dreams

Some people believe that they can control their dreams and many of us have recounted a dream with the words, 'it was strange, but I knew I was dreaming'. Lucid dreaming – when you know you are dreaming – is a useful technique to learn, particularly if you are prey to disturbing dreams or nightmares, as it enables your conscious mind to impose some sort of order on the dreamscape. Some theorists believe that lucid dreaming represses the unconscious, depriving it of the freedom to roam through the brain, thereby experiencing useful dreams. It is not an easy discipline to learn, but the following technique might help.

Scientific studies have noted that sleepers who are awakened in the middle of REM sleep are able to recall their dreams very clearly. If you want to try this, set your alarm clock to wake you 1.5–2 hours after you have fallen asleep.

Many people find that writing is an excellent way to unwind at the end of the day. A diary will help you to clarify the problems of the day and put them into some sort of perspective, allowing a peaceful transition to a night of untroubled sleep.

THREE STEPS TO LUCID DREAMING

- ⊙ Ask yourself repeatedly if you are dreaming; do this throughout the day and especially as you are dropping off to sleep. In this way, the question may insert itself into your dream.

- ⊙ As you fall asleep, tell yourself you will have at least one memorable dream, but that it will not be real, only a dream.

- ⊙ Set your alarm to wake you about an hour and a half into your sleep, when you should be in the middle of REM sleep. (This is not a technique to be recommended for those who share a bed!) Write down your dream when you wake up, then read a book before you go back to sleep. Tell yourself that you will have another memorable dream.

If you have a particular problem that you wish to address in a dream, try to incubate it into your dream and manipulate your dream to your will.

If you become frustrated by your inability to remember your dreams, try to make sure that you have a few nights' rest without worrying about them. Relax and enjoy sleep untroubled by the creeping realisation that you must record your thoughts on waking. The chances are that you will awake more refreshed and able to remember any dreams more clearly.

Recurring dreams

Many people experience the same dream over a period of weeks, months or even years, and recurring dreams are probably symptomatic of an existing problem that the unconscious is trying to resolve. Recurring dreams may reflect traumatic events years in the past, or they may mirror emotional problems. If you suffer from a recurring dream, ask yourself what else is happening in your life each time it recurs; in other words, what triggers it?

Recurring dreams are often triggered by conflicts and anxieties in the past.

A recurring dream may reflect past problems.

What message is the dream endeavouring to convey? Try to resolve the conflict or problem that the dream is addressing and it will probably disappear. Incidentally, recurring dreams seem to underline the importance of dreams to us all. If dreams are simply a collection of meaningless images, as some people believe, why do some of them recur? Random projections are surely unlikely to yield the same dream scenario month after month, even night after night.

Nightmares

Nightmares are simply disturbing or frightening dreams, the subject matter a projection of our own fears or frustration. The most basic form of nightmare, known as an incubus attack, is one in which the dreamer feels threatened by an unseen horror and feels suffocated or stifled. These dreams have no real meaning and, indeed, may have a physical basis: they might occur when the dreamer has difficulty breathing.

Nightmares that begin as narrative dreams and end with the dreamer in a state of distress are usually rooted in the problems, fears or stress of the dreamer's life. If they are persistent or really disturbing, the dreamer should consider consulting a dream therapist or seeking out a dream discussion group.

During the First World War the British doctor W H R Rivers (1864–1922) worked in the Royal Army Medical Corps treating shell-shocked patients at Craiglockhart mental hospital (the poet

While dream therapy is far from being a recognised medical discipline, certain schools of psychotherapy have acknowledged the importance of using dreams to help assess the mental state of a patient. Conventional western medicine has been slow to exploit the power of dreams, but many indigenous peoples such as Native American tribes or Tibetans have dream interpreters within their societies whom troubled dreamers can consult.

Siegfried Sassoon was among them). Many of his patients suffered appalling nightmares, accompanied by shrieking and sweating as they relived the conditions of the fighting in the trenches of France.

Sassoon's contemporary Wilfred Owen, himself no stranger to the trauma of the trenches, expressed most vividly the dreamers' utter vulnerability before the tenacious and ghastly images of war in his

'In all my dreams before my helpless sight

He plunges at me, guttering, choking, drowning.'

poem *Dulce et decorum est*:
However, as Rivers's patients recovered from their experiences, the bad dreams lessened and Rivers believed that the nightmares themselves were cathartic. He felt that dreams were a very primitive mechanism and also noted that children are more prone to nightmares than adults, perhaps because they cannot deal with their problems in a more sophisticated way.

Nightmares are often the product of an anxious mind, when the dreamer's problems and fears, which are suppressed during the day, manifest themselves as a terrifying dream, jerking the dreamer awake, wide-eyed with terror. Adults are usually able to calm themselves, but to children, such dreams seem very real.

In times of immense stress, such as war, even the dreams of non-combatants are often compensatory or wish fulfilment. The unconscious mind tries to compensate for the appalling daytime experiences and images of the dreamer's life with comforting images of home or loved ones. By contrast, once safe again, soldiers often suffer as they relive their combat experiences in their dreams.

Problem solving

Just as dreams can be useful in helping to solve emotional problems, they have also helped in more practical ways. Many people have struggled with a quiz or crossword question, gone to bed, 'slept on it' and woken up with the answer, as their brain has plucked the necessary information from the recesses of their mind while they were asleep. These impressive examples of the power of the sleeping mind are even more striking when one considers the famous examples of scientists and inventors who have benefited from their dreams. In 1844, for example, the inventor Elias Howe had reached an impasse with his design for a mechanical sewing machine and could not work out where to place the hole on the needle. One night he dreamt that Zulu warriors were throwing spears at him, although the spears were unusual because they had an eye-shaped hole at the tip. On waking he knew exactly where to put the hole on the machine's needle.

Simply writing down the bare bones of your dreams may help trigger your memories. Begin by using short one-word notes, of colours, sensations, people and scenarios.

This dream image, which reflects Michaelangelo's *The Creation of Adam*, may be about the transfer of power between two people, or signify communications and links between organisations.

The German chemist Friedrich Kekule (1829–96) studied the complex molecular construction of benzene, and although he knew it contained six atoms of carbon and six of hydrogen, he could not work out how they were joined together. One night in 1865 he dreamt that the atoms formed long rows that fitted neatly together and twisted and turned like snakes. One of the snakes suddenly grabbed its own tail and Kekule awoke with the solution to his problem: the benzene ring. He began a subsequent lecture with the words, 'Gentlemen, let us learn to dream', and went on to describe what he had seen. 'The atoms danced before my eyes... wriggling and turning like snakes. And see, what was that? One of the snakes seized its own tail, and the image whirled scornfully before my eyes. As though from a flash of lightning I awoke.'

Tips for Sweet Dreams

- Remember that nothing is quite what it seems—consider the symbolism of an object as well as its actual function.

- Dreams are usually composed of both literal and symbolic imagery. When interpreting a dream, consider what you were doing the day before, as the events of the day may recur in your dreams.

- The mind often uses puns and word games in dreams.

- Try to recall the colours of the dream landscape and the general shapes inherent in the dream – they may be important symbols.

- If you are threatened by dream monsters, turn and confront them – they will often disappear.

- Your physical condition may affect your dreams. While it is popularly believed that eating cheese gives you vivid dreams, it is more certain that going to bed hungry will lead to a disturbed night's sleep, and too much alcohol may induce intense dreams, sometimes of a nightmarish quality.

Turn to confront the monsters of your dreams, and you will probably see that they are merely shadows with no power to hurt you.

Total recall

Many people believe that they never dream, but the likelihood is that they simply don't remember, possibly because they always wake up during periods of non-REM sleep. Dreams are often intangible: fragments may recur, but the whole is often tantalisingly out of reach and, the harder one tries to remember, the more it slips away. As so much of what occurs in dreams seems bizarre in comparison with our waking experiences, it may be that the mind simply struggles to cope with the task of remembering illogical events and scenes. We undoubtedly forget the great majority of our dreams – which is perhaps just as well, given that the average person has between three and six dreams per night. Having said all that, most of what seems odd in the dream world can be related to your waking life if you examine your dreams properly.

A sample dream diary page is illustrated to help define your dream memories. If you photocopy it and keep a few beside your bed, you will be able to record your dreams as accurately and quickly as possible.

Fragments of dreams often stay with us throughout the day, but the rest remains elusive. Images are hazy, people's faces are unclear and the events are disconnected. One of the most frustrating things is waking in the middle of the night after a fantastic dream and being unable to recapture the feelings while falling back to sleep.

Dream diary

Time: _____

Main event yesterday: _____
_____
_____

Plans for today: _____
_____
_____

Brief synopsis of dream: _____
_____
_____

Feelings on awakening: _____
_____
_____

Type: (Ordinary, recurring, lucid,
predictive, nightmare, sexual, wish
fulfilment, visionary, other)
_____

Time: past, present, future,
    Day, night, midday, evening, dawn
    Season
    Childhood
    Historical
    Fantasy
    Other

Atmosphere _____

Dreamer's reaction/mood _____

Colours _____

Symbols _____

People _____

Animals _____

Objects _____

Places _____

Buildings _____

Words/puns _____

How to Remember Your Dreams

- Before you go to sleep, say to yourself 'I will remember my last dream'. Repeat this in your head rhythmically and in time with your breathing.

- Try to wake up slowly, allowing time to mull over the remnants of your dream.

- Keep a notebook and pencil next to your bed to note down key words and images about your dream as you wake up. Alternatively, use a tape recorder to record your thoughts on waking. Try to recall any predominant colours or shapes in addition to the basic plot, background and characters.

Meditation and deep breathing are excellent methods of relaxing properly before falling asleep. Try to forget about any troubles you may have encountered during the day and concentrate on breathing evenly.

- Later in the day, write up your dream in a dream diary as fully as possible. Date the entry, and include your emotions on waking – how the dream made you feel, whether you were puzzled by it or felt you knew exactly what it was about. By keeping a detailed dream diary, you will be able to examine the pattern of your dreams over time.

- Ask yourself basic questions about images and events of the dream. If you dream of scrubbing a large hall with a tiny toothbrush for example, notice why the toothbrush is significant – how it differs from a regular scrubbing brush. Contrast the dream imagery with the facts of real life to help you understand the dream more clearly.

'I have had a dream past the wit of man to say what dream it was', says Bottom in Shakespeare's *A Midsummer Night's Dream*. Bottom, of course, was overwhelmed by the strangeness of events (and how many people have dreamed of acquiring an ass's head?) but for most of us the frustration lies simply in trying to pin down the dream. Try to note down the essentials in the first ten minutes after waking; leave it any longer and the fundamentals are more likely to disappear.

The next phase is to try to understand your dreams, an activity that humankind has found fascinating for thousands of years. The son of the noted American psychic Edgar Cayce remarked that 'the most informative book you will ever read about dreams is the one you write yourself.' Understand that dreams are the products of each individual and that they reflect the hopes, fears and lifestyle of the dreamer. The important thing is to keep an open mind, and embrace the possibilities of your dreaming mind. As Geoffrey Chaucer wrote in *The House of Fame*,

'God turns to good all our dreams

For one great mystery, to me it seems,

Is how it is that dreams are born

Whether at evening or at morn,

And why it is that some come true,

While others never do...

...but if the causes of these miracles

Are known by someone better than I

Let him explain them.'

Chapter 1

The Big Sleep

'I talk of dreams
Which are the children of an idle brain,
Begot of nothing but vain fantasy'
Mercutio in *Romeo and Juliet*.

Although each of us is a unique individual, we are prey to similar anxieties and experiences in our waking lives, and these are reflected in our dreams. Dreams address the most important areas of our lives: relationships, work, our past and our hopes for the future, and can often help to solve problems or anxieties that crop up. As Artemidorus noted over 2,000 years ago, 'It is profitable – indeed, not only profitable but necessary – for the dreamer as well as the person who is interpreting, that the dream interpreter know the dreamer's identity, occupation, birth, financial status, state of health and age'. There are several dream themes that recur again and again throughout our lives, although the finer details will differ between individuals.

Our dreams reflect every part of our waking lives, work. . . and play.

Pursuit

Scientists in sleep laboratories have established that the body experiences immense physiological reactions during REM sleep, not least the adrenaline surge that accompanies fear and the feeling that we need to escape. Dreams about chasing or being chased provoke emotions ranging from fear to exhilaration to pure terror.

Some dreams are just the mind's way of working through the events of the day, and many dreams about places of work come into this category.

If you have ever experienced a dream in which you were being pursued, you may remember the unsettling feelings of persecution and disorientation lingering on after waking up. Dreams of being chased are among the most common anxiety dreams and I remember a particularly disturbing version of being hunted across war-torn 1940s Europe during which I felt very afraid. The wartime scenario was probably related to some research I was involved in and the feeling of pursuit to the stress of meeting a deadline.

Perhaps I felt that my work was chasing me across other areas of my life.

If you suffer from pursuit dreams try to confront whatever is chasing you and try to overcome the fear you feel; these dreams often reflect some sort of conflict in the dreamer's life. Perhaps you are running away from something or someone, or you feel pressurised or stressed by a situation. If so, try to untangle the strands of your life so that you prioritise what is important

Destination
unavailable

Dreams in which the dreamer has to travel interminably to reach an appointment or unspecified destination are classic anxiety dreams and are very common. Usually a succession of trains, planes and cars fail to connect, break down or behave in any number of unlikely ways to prevent the dreamer getting to where he knows he should be. These are dreams of pointless journeys in which the dreamer has to react to events and feels he has no control over what is happening. They reflect the frustrations and anxieties of everyday life and often feature friends or relatives either helping or hindering the dream journey. These can be exhausting dreams and leave one feeling irritated by the sheer waste of time. On one level these dreams usually indicate that the dreamer feels stressed by the demands of working and family life, and feels that he or she never quite succeeds in everything they set out to do. On a deeper level, this type of dream may reflect low self-esteem; the ambitions of the dream, and perhaps those in life, are not realised and it may be time to re-evaluate your lifestyle.

If you dream about a road, your dream may reflect your feelings about your progress through life. A long road with clear views implies that the dreamer is happy with how their life is unfolding, but a rocky road strewn with obstacles shows that the dreamer feels that something or someone is blocking their progress.

Someone
to watch over you

Public exposure can be very humiliating and dreams in which the dreamer is caught doing something that would normally be confined to the privacy and comfort of a bedroom or bathroom reflect this basic human fear. Such dreams include being watched while on the lavatory, or being naked in public and leave the dreamer with a feeling of shame long after waking up, as though the subconscious wanted to reinforce the embarrassment felt in the dream. These dreams are about shame, insecurity and the public face we present to the world; ask yourself if you are hiding something from friends or family.

Falling

How many times have you drifted off to sleep, only to wake with a jerk as though you were falling? This is the result of muscle spasms relaxing into sleep, and such dreams are characterised by quite a strong sensation of falling through space, whether it be from an aircraft, over a cliff edge or from the roof of your house. Although caused by muscle spasms, a recurrence of falling dreams may signify that one area of your life seems to be beyond your control. No

one can exert any control over a fall and a dream like this should encourage the dreamer to examine his or her life and consider whether they are shaping events or simply reacting to decisions made for them by others. Are they being pushed over the edge?

Flying

Birds are free to fly wherever they wish, unconstrained by borders or regulations.

Dreams in which one soars over the earth like a bird are exhilarating and may act as compensation for a feeling of inferiority in life. Two thousand years ago Artemidorus succinctly noted, 'To fly is to be lifted above those about one', and flying dreams enable the dreamer to acquire a different perspective on life, literally 'rising above' obstacles placed in the way of his aspirations. Some theorists believe that flying dreams are linked to out-of-body experiences, when the soul goes travelling while the body sleeps, and dreamers usually say that they feel remarkably optimistic and refreshed after a flying dream. Consider the context of the dream and see whether it reflects your actions in life: are you trying to 'rise above' a problem, 'flying in the face of fortune', or 'flying off the handle'?

Looking down on a scene from a great height gives one a different perspective on events.

Water

Dream analysts relate water to the dreamer's emotional life, partly because psychologists link it with the amniotic fluid we all swam in inside our mothers' wombs. In fact, Freud believed it represented a desire to return to the comforting world of the womb. Water can appear in dreams in many ways: as the sea, a swimming pool, a bath, as drinking water or as a flood, for example. Dreams of waterfalls or of being carried along a torrent of water may hark back to the dreamer's birth, as some analysts believe that memory of our birth experience lingers on in our subconscious. The meaning of water in

Swimming represents the personal effort involved in dealing with our emotions. Just as swimmers constantly battle to stay afloat in water, so mentally healthy individuals must examine their emotional life and work to address any problems.

Waterfalls are often very beautiful, yet the majesty of the sheet of dropping water masks the danger they pose to river crafts. If you dream about going over the edge of a waterfall, you probably feel that you are about to take some sort of risk with your emotional life.

If you dream about a river, try to remember the condition of the water as it reflects your emotional state. A clear river that contains fish reflects a contented and alert person, while a muddy stagnant river implies that the dreamer is unhappy.

the dream varies enormously depending on the form it takes and the dreamer's relationship to it. Gazing at a peaceful, blue lake is rather different from struggling against the waves in a rough sea, for example. Sometimes, dreamers are faced with a lake or river, which they know they must cross before they can progress; this often represents an important transition in the dreamer's life, such as adapting to a new situation after divorce or bereavement.

If you find yourself in a boat on a river, this may signify the path of your life: are you in control of the craft, or do you feel frightened of the rapids ahead? Dreams of floating peacefully in a deep,

blue sea leave dreamers feeling relaxed and restored and are among the most comforting dream scenarios. If water represents the emotions, this type of dream shows a happy and confident dreamer, secure in his surroundings.

Boats appear in many guises and sometimes symbolise the dreamer. If this is the case, the type of craft and its condition are important: are you a majestic open-going yacht, a tramp steamer or a powerful speedboat?

Dreams in which the water is rough or appears to be strewn with obstacles reflect a less settled emotional life, while stagnant water suggests an unhealthy, even dead emotional life. A flood usually symbolises some sort of emotional crisis – feelings which have been repressed or held in check suddenly gush forth, leaving the dreamer surprised by their power. This kind of dream often occurs at a significant time in one's life, such as a death, or a major job change. Take note of your attitude to the water in your dream: are you happy to dive in, or do you feel reluctant to immerse yourself? If you hold back from the dream water, there may some aspect of your emotional life that you do not want to address (see pages 158–161).

A dream about waves does not always mean that you are experiencing serious trouble, but perhaps that your life or work has become more challenging. It is always possible to ride out waves if you are prepared for them, so use this metaphor to equip yourself for choppy times ahead.

Death

Dreams about death, either one's own or that of someone close, are inevitably unnerving and can leave you feeling that you have experienced some sort of precognitive vision. This is unlikely, but it cannot be ruled out. Dreams featuring conversations with dead people are also common and can be comforting to the bereaved; they are probably a subconscious way of coping with the grieving process.

Death can be considered either symbolically or on a more straightforward level and its interpretation will depend on the circumstances of the dreamer. In symbolic terms, death marks the end of one phase and the beginning of another. A dream about your own death may symbolise a desire to retreat from the pressures of life, and Artemidorus noted that 'To dream of death is good for those in fear, for the dead have no more fears'.

Dreaming of the death of someone close may help the dreamer prepare for an event that is inevitable, or may represent some sort of antagonism towards them. Dreams of long-dead relatives or friends often occur at a time when the dreamer feels the need for guidance or advice from a trusted source.

Gravestones inevitably lend a macabre tone to a dream, especially if the tomb features the dreamer's name: it is this sort of dream that often causes a sudden awakening and leaves the dreamer feeling distinctly unsettled. Gravestones may symbolise the need for the dreamer to bury an aspect of his life or work.

Sex

Everyone dreams about love and romance, even people in happy stable relationships. Although former US President Jimmy Carter famously declared that even looking at another woman was tantamount to adultery, dream lovers are generally harmless fantasies that enliven our dreams.

Freud believed that all dreams related to sex, and while this view has been largely discredited, there is no doubt that people dream about sex fairly regularly. Reasons for this vary: the dreamer may be compensating in his dream life for the lack of sexual activity in his waking life, or the dreamer may be dissatisfied with his or her partner. Dreams about sex with partners whom one would normally regard as inappropriate are not necessarily the expression of a subconscious urge, but may just be related to the fact that you saw them during the day and they have somehow intruded into your dream! Fantasies about torrid sex with pin-up celebrities are obviously wish fulfilment and an excellent reason to train in the art of lucid dreaming (see page 34). On a more serious level, perhaps your dreams are one way of encouraging you to examine your relationship with your partner, to check that you are both happy and fulfilled.

Royalty

A staggeringly large percentage of people report dreaming about the Queen or royalty. The symbolism of the royal family is probably more important than the individuals themselves in most dreams: they are archetypal figures of authority, wealth and glamour. A crown is an ancient symbol of authority worn by emperors, kings and princes for innumerable generations. Encrusted with jewels, crowns also symbolise wealth, power and an element of aloofness as they set the owners apart from others.

Incredibly, large numbers of the British population report dreams which feature the Queen or members of the royal family. The Queen's head is almost ubiquitous, of course, as it appears on stamps and coins, and she is a figure of great dignity, representing stability, power, wealth and authority. What is more surprising, however, is that many people dream about entertaining the Queen in the familiar surroundings of their own home, which is probably less palatial than those to which Elizabeth II is accustomed. Such dreams are partly a reflection of the times in which we live: the media is constantly trying to establish that royalty are 'just like you and I', and although the Queen appears extremely familiar, she remains rather aloof. Unless the dreamer is a keen royalist (in which case this is a wish-fulfilment dream), he or she may be trying to exert some control over the authority the Queen represents, or may need to confront someone in a position of power about an aspect of their life which they feel is restricted.

Paralysis

Most people, however confident they appear in everyday life, are prey to doubts and worries at some point. They may fear that they are being stifled creatively or are merging facelessly into a crowd with their individualism crushed. Such fears may manifest themselves as anxiety dreams. Professional or work-related worries are more likely to produce insomnia, but even when the stressed person has fallen asleep, their dreams may not be entirely relaxing.

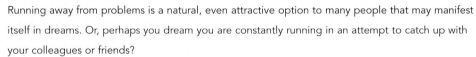

Running away from problems is a natural, even attractive option to many people that may manifest itself in dreams. Or, perhaps you dream you are constantly running in an attempt to catch up with your colleagues or friends?

Although vital functions continue while we dream, during Rapid Eye Movement (REM) sleep the limbs are immobile and paralysed to prevent the dreamer carrying out the actions he or she is dreaming about. Actual dreams about paralysis or the inability to move are very common, however, and are classic anxiety dreams. The scenario varies, but may feature a dream in which the dreamer is threatened by someone or something, and is unable to run away. Or, having seen a person teetering on the edge of a cliff, the dreamer feels unable to leap forward and grab them. These dreams reflect a lack of confidence in some area of our waking lives, and may occur during times of stress, particularly where there is a reluctance to make changes. They may also reflect the feeling that you are rooted to one place while friends or family are moving on around you. Perhaps there is an area of your life that you find frustrating, in which case you must consider making changes to address the problem.

Chapter 2
The Building Blocks

'Dreams are faithful interpreters of our inclinations; but there is art required to sort and understand them.'

(Montaigne 'Of Experience' in Essays 1580–88)

The Roman interpreter Artemidorus wrote, 'Dreams and visions are infused into men for their advantage and instruction', but before you can begin to interpret dreams properly, it is helpful to have some knowledge of the rudimentary symbols that occur in the dreams of most people. Dreams are primarily visual, but the images are often based on word play, puns or common sayings.

Carl Jung was the first dream analyst to identify what he called the 'collective unconscious', an assortment of symbols and images common to cultures throughout the world. He studied the folklore, history and religion of many different peoples and believed that everyone, irrespective of their background, inherits an ancestral memory, a myth-producing part of the unconscious mind which houses the primordial images common to the dreams of us all. Similarly, we are influenced by symbols and shapes we

The altar at Stonehenge is illuminated by the sun.

see around us during our waking hours; the most obvious, perhaps is the Christian cross, or a crescent moon for Moslems. Jung believed that an individual's psychological make-up had three levels: the collective unconscious of ancestral memories; the personal unconscious consisting of an individual's hopes and fears; and the conscious mind. Dreams draw their themes and images from all three levels, but remember that any person or object in a dream landscape may simply have meanings relevant to the dreamer alone.

The cross is one of the clearest religious symbols in the world.

Archetypes

Jungian dream analysts and psychologists believe that the collective unconscious is made up of several components of the human psyche, otherwise known as 'archetypes'. Everybody presents a public face to the world, which often masks true feelings: Jung called this archetype the 'persona' and it is balanced by the 'shadow' archetype – that part of our character we keep hidden, sometimes, even denying certain characteristics to ourselves.

A shadowy, menacing figure in dreams, therefore, may represent that part of ourselves that we find hard to face, the mean-minded, brutal, miserable side that is best kept hidden. The best example of this is in Robert Louis Stevenson's novel, *The Strange Case of Dr Jekyll and Mr Hyde*. (Interestingly, Stevenson attributed many of his plots and inspirations to his dreams, saying he was helped in his sleep by the little people, whom he referred to as 'brownies'.) Dreams featuring the dreamer wearing a mask also infer that

The appearance of a masked individual in a dream emphasises that aspects of the dreamer's personality are obscured in some way. Perhaps the dreamer feels that he or she is forced to wear a mask, or cannot remove it: if this is the case, the real personality is probably being buried.

the dreamer wants to remain anonymous or unrecognised.

Jung coined the terms 'anima' and 'animus' to encompass the qualities of the opposite sex, which exist in us all. The animus is the embodiment of

Most people would admit that the image they present to the world often hides anger, disappointment or frustration. Sometimes we are confronted in our dreams by the very emotions, such as anger, for example, we are trying to hide from those around us and it may be the unconscious mind's way of allowing free rein to those feelings.

masculine characteristics – independence, confidence and practicality – while the anima are the feminine, intuitive qualities. Everyone must balance their male and female qualities so that the 'Self', the dreamer's personality, can be healthy and achieve its potential, something Jung called 'individuation'. The anima may appear in the dreams of a man who has been neglecting the caring or 'feminine' side of his personality. Similarly, the animus may appear in women's dreams to encourage confidence or analytical judgement.

A man who neglects his anima may become overbearing, aggressive and harsh, and as an archetype it usually takes the form of a woman a man has known all his life, such as his mother. A woman who embraces her animus will be independent, self-sufficient and articulate, but if she ignores her masculine side, may become insecure and clingy; an animus often appears in dreams as a woman's father.

There are four further male and female archetypes, each representing two complementary sides of a personality, or the Self. They can feature in the dreams of everyone. Female archetypes are the Great Mother (or Mother Earth) figure, the nurturing, loving ideal mother; the negative side of this is the Terrible Mother, a possessive, vengeful figure who can stifle independence. The second is the Princess, the eternally youthful and sexy female figure who governs love and relationships and incorporates qualities of consideration, spontaneity and vivaciousness. Her shadow is the Siren, capricious, seductive and ultimately doomed. The Amazon represents the female intellect

The image of a mother and son is one of the most comforting possible within a dream: the child dreams of the person who probably loves him unconditionally, and the mother sees an innocent, lovable child, unsullied by the cynicism of adulthood.

Motherhood is not always easy and many mothers lack the serenity accorded to the archetypal image of the earth mother. The archetypal image of the 'terrible mother' is depicted here in a milder form of the angry woman.

and may appear in dreams as a professional woman – a doctor or lawyer, for example. The Huntress is the shadow of the Amazon, an embittered figure, constantly striving, but forever frustrated. The Priestess stands for intuition and spirituality, a wise figure whose negative side is the Witch. All these figures can manifest themselves in dreams as familiar characters, but their archetypal qualities are clear.

TABLE SHOWING POSITIVE AND NEGATIVE DREAM ARCHETYPES

Quality	Great Mother		Great Father	
Aspect	**positive**	**negative**	**positive**	**negative**
Intellect	Mother	Terrible Mother	Wise Man	Ogre
Emotion	Princess	Siren	Prince	Wastrel
Practicality	Amazonian	Huntress	Warrior	Villain
Intuition	Priestess	Witch	Priest	Black Magician

The male equivalents are the Wise Old Man, or father figure – often a source of advice or authority in dreams. His opposite is the Ogre, a cruel paternalistic figure, often menacing and powerful. The dreamer's perceptions of his own father will contribute strongly to the construction of these figures. The younger male archetype is the Prince, an idealistic figure who may be searching for wisdom. His search may deteriorate and simply go astray, transforming the Prince into his alter ego the Wastrel or tramp, a perpetual drifter. The Hero or Warrior embodies qualities of ambition, bravery and attractiveness, whereas the Villain is a selfish, sometimes aggressive egotist. The Priest embodies male spirituality and guidance, whereas his shadow, the Black Magician is a sinister, manipulative figure.

Whenever a strong male or female character appears in a dream, particularly if it is an unfamiliar person, ask yourself what that character represents, as they may incorporate a message from the subconscious. Familiar people in dreams are more likely to be appearing as themselves.

Neither sex can afford to neglect the masculine side of their character. These images symbolise the best characteristics of the animus: the paternal and wise father figure, the brave hero, the spiritual and generous-spirited priest and the innocent child.

Colours

Most people dream in colour, although some people believe that their dreams are monochrome; many researchers believe that heightened or especially bright colours in a dream may be a sign of a precognitive dream. If your dream has been dominated by one colour, you should regard it as a separate symbol. We are surrounded by colour all the time, every day, and we associate certain colours with different people, places and festivals.

Red is the colour of heat, fire, energy and passion; it often warns of coming danger or it may reflect anger. If red is a predominant colour in your dream, consider your energy levels – are you blazing away at something and tiring yourself out?

Green is almost the opposite of red, both in the colour spectrum and in terms of its meaning. Scientists believe it is the most relaxing colour and it can symbolize fertility, new life and optimism. Green is also the colour associated with environmental issues. However, phrases such as 'green with jealousy' should not be ignored, so if you have a green dream, examine your relationships, or consider whether you are feeling jealous of another's achievements.

Yellow and gold are associated with the sun, optimism and glory. Gold is the colour of wealth and royalty. A yellow dream might be encouraging you to pursue your ambitions. A murky yellow may herald an illness, or perhaps you feel 'jaundiced' and dissatisfied about a situation.

Silver is a mystical colour, which can denote purity. The light of the silvery moon may illuminate a problem, so silver can be the colour of insight and wisdom; it also relates to the night. It may also refer to money.

Blue ('moody blue') signifies our emotions and moods. The colour of the sky, it relates to our spiritual side and intellect. In Christian symbolism, it is the colour of the Virgin Mary's robes and indicates chastity, peace and happiness. Dark blue, the colour of the sea probably relates to deep-seated emotions; you may be feeling nostalgic or depressed, or possibly confused about something, literally 'all at sea'.

Purple relates to authority, religion and intuition. Purple was an imperial colour during the Roman Empire, and is still used for religious vestments and royal robes, so consider whether you have been acting regally. 'Purple prose' is a phrase about exaggeration – has your behaviour been a little over the top?

In Western tradition, white represents purity, light and innocence. Brides wear white as a symbol of their virginity. In Eastern tradition, the colour is associated with mourning and death. A bright white light is often associated with God or a powerful life force in dreams.

Black is the opposite of white; it marks a lack of colour and light, and thus the absence of God; a black dreamscape is profoundly gloomy and scary. Associated with depression, fear and secrecy, black usually expresses the wicked side of human nature and often is associated with mourning in Western cultures.

Brown is the colour of the earth and of nature; our well-being is rooted in the richness of the soil, and the colour can refer to honesty and simplicity. It is also seen as a dull colour, and Freud related it to excreta.

Jewels

Diamonds, the purest and most brilliant of precious stones, generally indicate happiness and prosperity, unless someone else is wearing them, in which case, the dreamer is probably envious of a friend or colleague's good fortune. A dream about being given diamonds signifies a recognition of your worth and achievements. Emeralds are a piercing green – the colour of jealousy

Precious stones may appear in dreams, their meaning associated with their colours, their value and the particular symbolism of each stone. We value jewels, so they may simply represent our desire to look after the things we treasure, such as family, home and possessions. The appearance of large numbers of jewels may simply be a wish-fulfilment dream about acquiring wealth and happiness, or it may have more subtle nuances.

A dream about being given jewels shows a desire for recognition and a need for your qualities to be rewarded. If you dream you are the generous-hearted donor, it shows that you are able to recognise the value of your friends.

Diamond rings have an especial symbolism in that they are traditionally used as engagement rings, the hardness of the diamond intended to symbolise the firmness of the couple's commitment to one another.

Ireland is a lush country, the sheer greenness of the landscape caused by plentiful rainfall, which has led to the nickname the 'Emerald Isle'. In dreams, Ireland may be populated by leprechauns.

– and may hint at a rival in love. Associations with Ireland (the 'Emerald Isle') may herald a Celtic connection. Rubies are a deep red, a feminine colour, (the Bible notes that a virtuous woman's price is 'far above rubies') which is also the colour of the heart, so the appearance of a ruby in a dream means luck in love, gambling or business. If you dream that you have lost a ruby, you may subconsciously want to lose a lover. The 'true blue' of sapphires hints that the dreamer may find the right partner.

Opals are the chameleons of precious stones, their hues altering with the light, so their appearance in dreams is not a good sign. Traditionally, they are regarded as immensely unlucky if used for an engagement ring. The creamy opulence of a string of pearls depicts a great social life, money and fun. Individual pearls are found hidden in oyster shells, so are highly prized and hint at a secret life, confidences and undiscovered treasure. Pearls are perfect spheres that have evolved naturally and almost miraculously from a grain of sand, so their endurance often represents love and relationships.

The red of rubies is reminiscent of passion and love, although if a woman dreams about losing a ruby, it implies that her lover has become indifferent to her. It may also refer to a woman of that name.

Numbers

1 9
3 11
5 13
7 15
17

2 10
4 12
6 14
8 16
18

Numbers appear in many guises in dreams, and can signify something as mundane as a telephone number, a date, the number of people you were with at dinner or the cost of a bar of chocolate. More symbolically a number can represent the Holy Trinity. In dreams the number may be important but the dream item less so; for example, a dream which mentions 25 miles may remind the dreamer that in reality, he owes a friend £25. Numbers can incorporate intensely personal meanings or archetypal ones, so consider both possibilities. Traditionally, odd numbers are male and even numbers are female and many ancient belief systems set great store by them. The Mayans, for example, turned ordinary numbers into gods and numerology is important in divination and magic rituals.

Zero is nothing, a void that cannot be filled. The circle it forms is the Universe before life was created; it is also associated with the revolution of the Earth and planets around the sun. The number one is the basis of all numbers; it represents one person, isolation and, owing to its phallic shape, the power of masculinity. In religious symbolism it means one god.

Two is concerned with balance, pairs, opposites or choices. Because two is associated with duality, or the fact that there are two sides to a problem, the dreamer may feel guided to examine a dilemma at length before making a decision.

Three is a holy digit, the number of the Trinity in Christian and Hindu beliefs, and of mythological figures like the Three Graces, or the Three Furies (not to mention the Three Stooges or the Three Degrees in 20th century culture). Phrases such as 'three's a crowd', may relate to feelings of exclusion in a dream.

Four is stable number representing solidity and the Earth. The four points of the compass, the four gospels and four elements all hint at dependability and balance, and four can relate to a square and the cross.

Five is a magic number with references to the pentacle and five-pointed star. It also represents humans (with four limbs and a head, as well as five digits on hands and feet) and can mean creativity.

Six relates to the Creation – it took six days for God to create the Earth – and to sex, which can be symbolised by an upward and downward triangle superimposed on top of one another. Druids regard the number six as especially holy.

Seven is a mystical number in many cultures, partly because it seems rooted in nature; On the seventh day, God rested after creating the earth, so it is a number associated with God and accomplishment; there are seven days in the week, seven colours in a rainbow and Seven Wonders of the World. There are also seven deadly sins.

Eight has no great significance in Western civilisation, but Buddhists believe in an eight-fold path to enlightenment. If the numeral eight is turned on its side, it becomes a lemniscate, the symbol of infinity. Eight is also associated with a mariner's rose, the compass drawn with the four intermediate points in addition to the usual cardinal points, and which also looks like the spokes of a wheel. Eight may be regarded as a numeral of balance and symmetry, although many analysts believe it appears rarely in dreams.

Nine is the last single-digit number and is thus associated with endings. Pregnancy lasts nine months, so it may be an indication of creativity or exciting projects. The numeral ten is interesting as it incorporates the single, phallic figure one and the encompassing female circle of creation, the zero.

Ten is the number of rules and regulations: the decimal system is based on ten, and there are Ten Commandments. Eleven, two ones together, represents intuition; the two figures, which reflect the Self, symbolise self-knowledge and perception. Twelve is another important numeral, a cyclic number rooted in the changing seasons and the passage of time: there are twelve numbers on a clock face, twelve months in the year and twelve signs of the zodiac. It is also an important number in the imperial system of measurement. Thirteen is associated with bad luck in Western culture, a superstition relating to the fact that there were thirteen diners at Christ's Last Supper, and one of them, Judas, betrayed Him.

Other numbers are rooted in everyday life and their meaning will be clear to the dreamer; for example, digits such as 999 or 911, the telephone numbers of the emergency services in many parts of the world. Since the terrorist attacks on the World Trade Centre in New York on 11 September 2001 (9/11/01) this particular number has taken on a new and terrible significance.

Shapes

In the days before mass literacy, symbolic shapes were an important means of non-verbal communication and, even today, road signs incorporate simple shapes to direct or warn drivers. A fish or cross represents Christianity, while circles and eggs embody both new life and the Universe itself. Sometimes you may emerge from a dream with the details missing, but one single image remaining in your mind; it may be an indication of the shape you are in – the shape of your circumstances. Look for simple formations in your dream landscapes and consider the meaning of them: if you can interpret the strong shapes that appear in your dreams you may be able to unravel the dream's message.

Eggs are the source of life and the cosmic egg, a variation of the circle, is the source of life. They are traditionally female symbols and are associated with the eternal cycle of birth, life, death and re-birth.

The symbolism of basic shapes such as circles is shared among widely different cultures across the world and features in the creation myths of many societies, the shape obviously drawn from the sun, the primordial source or energy and heat.

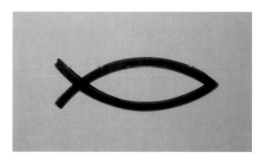

Christ was a 'fisher of men', and this simple line drawing is a clear representation of Christian belief.

A SHAPE DREAM

I walked out of the front door of our old house (although strangely the door was hung the wrong way) to see a lovely view of sun-dappled grass and fields and, in the distance, the chimneys and towers of houses I knew to be those of my friends. Our neighbours' house stood out because on the four corners of the tall wall surrounding it, they had placed what appeared to be flat-topped plastic white cones, rather like disposable cups. I walked in the other direction and looked out over the sea from a grassy cliff. The tide was going out exposing a stony island, which was exactly the same shape as the cones.

Interpretation: the sun, grass and lovely views gave this dream a nostalgic and happy atmosphere, which is pretty much how I see our old home. The repetition of the cone shapes may be important: the island appeared solid and reassuring, whereas the plastic cones appeared tacky. They are similar in shape to Aztec or Mayan pyramids, which often represent a need to connect with spiritual matters or aims, and the appearance of the solid island is in contrast to the almost disposable nature of the plastic cones. The island represents stability and long-standing aspirations, whereas the plastic cones symbolise the temporary attractions of modern, but more superficial ambitions.

The symbolism of basic, shapes such as circles, is shared among widely different cultures across the world and features in the creation myths of many societies, the shape obviously drawn from the sun, the primordial source or energy and heat.

The circle is the most simple dream image; it is associated with halos and thus purity and goodness. It may also represent the Earth. If filled with lines or another shape, it is called a 'mandala' and is similar to the diagrams used by Tibetan monks as a focus for prayers. An unadorned circle may also stand for the wheel of life. In dreams, circles are often associated with anxiety about social or family situations. Being outside a circle of friends or away from the family may induce unease; breaking out of a circle, or gaining independence is also tricky.

Variations on this theme include the egg, the symbol of new life or new beginnings, fertility and regeneration. Eggs may also appear as a pun and represent wealth, as in a nest egg, or imply embarrassment, as in having egg on one's face. Newly crowned monarchs carry a spherical orb, which signifies not only power, but also the kingdom cradled in their hand and the hope of the people for a successful reign. Rings have obvious associations with engagements and marriage, and signify loyalty and fidelity. If you dream you are given a ring, it is probably a good sign that your relationship with a friend or loved one is secure. If you lose a ring, however, this may symbolise a lack of commitment on the dreamer's part to an existing relationship.

The goose who laid the golden egg is a popular nursery tale, and this type of image most obviously refers to wealth or a 'nest egg'.

Pyramids point towards heaven, yet their broad bases are firmly rooted on earth. They often symbolise ambitions.

dreamer. Five-pointed stars are magical signs of protection. Stars may symbolise fate or destiny; 'follow your star' in your dreams and you may be surprised at what you discover. Sparkling stars in the night sky represent ambition or aspiration, particularly those of an artistic or intellectual nature.

Triangles indicate fire and spirituality, and equilateral triangles represent proportion and balance. They are related to the three-fold nature of man and the balance between body, soul and spirit. Pointing upwards to heaven, triangles express a striving for spiritual peace and may appear in really important dreams. Triangles appear in dreams as pyramids, huts or roof shapes.

Star shapes are formed by two triangles; a six-pointed star formed by one triangle pointing up and the other down, represents the union between the physical and spiritual sides of the

Both stars and pentagrams have acquired magical associations and are apparently used to cast spells or act as protective amulets. The five-pointed star is also regarded as the symbol of man, seen most clearly in Leonardo da Vinci's drawing of a naked man within a circle.

These business colleagues have contracted a 'square deal' to their mutual satisfaction.

Squares are solid, balanced shapes, which embody security – the dreamer has both feet firmly rooted to the ground. An enclosed shape, it may also represent imprisonment or a feeling of claustrophobia in a situation or relationship. We speak of facing a problem 'squarely', or standing 'four-square', or carrying out 'square deals', so it is associated with honesty. The diamond is a variation on the square and in Jungian analysis typifies the Self, with a well-balanced combination of male and female qualities.

Complex yet beautiful forms, spirals represent energy and movement; the double helix, the shape of DNA, characterises the continuity of the generations, the life force moving through humanity. Spirals may appear in dreams as creepers tumbling down from a tree, on shells, as ropes or as snakes. They are related to labyrinths, mazes and puzzles, and as such are to do with exploration, often of the soul.

This spiral spells confusion and anxiety, the dreamer perhaps worrying that events are spiralling out of control.

Geometrical shapes are the building blocks of life, nature and everything around us. In dreams shapes may simply refer to the object they form, or they may have a deeper meaning related to spiritual, emotional or unconscious feelings. When considering the shape of your dreamscape, take nothing at face value and always try to work out whether particularly memorable or strong shapes hold any extra meaning.

Solid, rigid and perfect for supports, squares may represent security. They appear in dreams as objects such as bricks, tables, gardens, rooms or courtyards, or perhaps as bare cells, when they can stand for incarceration.

Everyday objects

Mirrors are often endowed with magical qualities in fairy tales – witness the evil queen's mirror in *Snow White*, or Harry Potter's 'Mirror of Erised'. They are inextricably linked with appearance – what we would like to see as well as what is really before our eyes. The same may be true in dreams, so when you confront a dream mirror, prepare yourself for a surprise.

Windows allow outsiders to look in on activities within a house or another room, yet as they are solid objects, they also exclude the viewer from participation. Shuttered or curtained windows on a house are not welcoming and may reflect a dreamer's desire to retreat from the world around him or her.

Everyday objects also feature in dreams, although they may be distorted, over- or under-sized or simply used for the wrong purpose. They are instantly recognizable and may seem irrelevant to the dream environment. They may have a particular meaning to the dreamer or hold an archetypal symbolism, perhaps because of their shape or cultural or mythical connotations.

Mirrors reflect light and images, although in dreams mirrors often reflect something unexpected, which may also be important. Traditional dream interpreters believed that mirror dreams indicated misfortune or the loss of either money or friends. They may also emphasise the dreamer's vanity or concern with outward appearances. A cracked mirror symbolises emotional problems or an unwillingness to confront them.

Like mirrors, glass is easily broken; it is a solid object, yet it is transparent, so it is both a barrier and a window separating the dreamer from activities on the other side of it. A dream about smashing a window may represent the dreamer's frustration or feelings of exclusion from life on the other side of the glass. Drinking glasses can, proverbially be half empty or half full, and one's description of them reflects one's outlook on life. Glasses are often smashed after solemn toasts so that the glass cannot be used for a more mundane purpose, so a broken glass in dreams offers the possibility that your dreams will come true.

Similarly, full cups denote prosperity and empty ones represent losses; there may also be a pun, such as 'my cup runneth over'. Cups are classic female sexual symbols, and may feature in a more archetypal dream as a man searches for his 'holy grail', in other words the perfect woman. Jugs are traditional signs of virginity, so a broken or cracked jug suggests that someone is not as pure as they claim. Bottles can be regarded as representing the womb (they share a narrow entrance and a wider body), so a dream about trying to

Cups and glasses may appear as symbols of conviviality, a sign that a party is in full swing. A dream about broken glasses may represent the shattering of ideals or hopes.

fill a bottle may be sexual. Alternatively, the dreamer may be 'bottling up' emotions or feelings.

Clocks, watches, hourglasses or sundials all suggest a preoccupation with time moving on, or perhaps reflect a fear of growing old. They often appear grossly distorted in anxiety dreams to add to the stress the dreamer feels. Ticking may hint at the beating of a heart and reminds us that time is running out. A dream about a clock or watch in which the hands whiz around too fast suggests that the dreamer is highly stressed or emotionally charged.

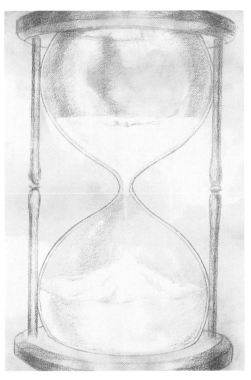

The sand which passes through an hourglass is a very obvious sign of time running out.

If you consult a sundial in your dream, ask yourself why you are using that rather than a more modern timepiece. It may reflect a preoccupation with the past that makes you neglect the present.

Candles were once used to mark the passage of time, and metaphors such as 'burning the candle at both ends' reflect this. Sources of illumination, they burn for a short time, but they also shed light on darkness and represent wisdom. An unlit candle symbolises missed opportunities. Candles are also phallic symbols, and a man's dream of a candle with a guttering flame, may reflect concerns regarding his potency.

Containers such as boxes or chests may be regarded as female sexual images, but more often they appear in dreams where they hide something the dreamer wishes to keep locked away from prying eyes. Freud suggested that boxes signify the womb and the

A room full of boxes hints at a house move and a feeling of dislocation, whereas a pile of brightly wrapped boxes is a delightful sight because it is a reminder of birthdays or Christmas and a time of gifts.

Candles can have ecclesiastical symbolism, as they are frequently seen in churches.

security associated with that. Empty boxes may express a lack of ambition or a feeling that life has dealt another disappointment.

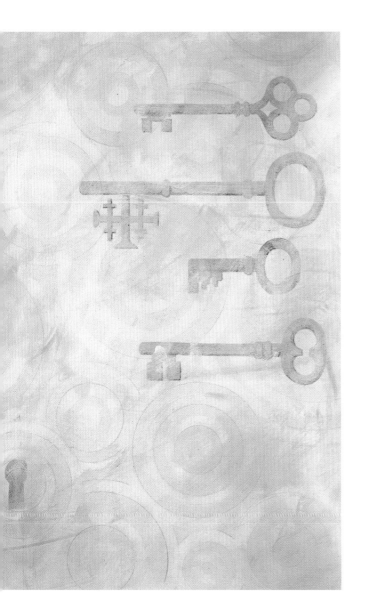

Keys are important symbolic objects which imply freedom, trust and status.

Keys are used to unlock boxes and the Freudian symbolism of placing a key (a phallic symbol) in a lock is fairly obvious. Artemidorus associated keys with love, noting that 'a key in a dream to him which would marry signifieth a good and handsome wife'. There are several metaphors about problem solving that relate to keys: 'finding the key to the problem', or gaining 'the keys to the kingdom', so keys often represent finding the solution to a problem. A dream about losing a key indicates disappointment, failure, even the loss of a friend, while being given a key denotes responsibility. If you dream about locking things up you may be repressing feelings about something, locking them away until you can bear to examine them. If you dream you are looking through a keyhole, you must ask yourself why you are away from the main action and why you need to spy on people.

In a dream, the kind of bag used to store your possessions may reflect your self-esteem or feelings of self-worth. Thus a set of matching Louis Vuiton luggage belongs to a confident dreamer, while a tatty plastic carrier bag suggests that the dreamer has lower self-esteem, or places little value on material possessions.

Bags and baggage reflect possessions – material, spiritual, emotional or intellectual. Thus an empty bag signifies a rather empty life and the dreamer is probably depressed. Perhaps it is time to go shopping to refill those empty bags. We all accumulate 'baggage' as we go through life. Some of it may be 'excess baggage' and should perhaps be shed in order to travel light. Bags also hide items from view, or can be used to store things for the future. If you dream about losing your baggage, try to pinpoint exactly what you fear is lost.

Baskets have related symbolism, although they are rigid containers and do not hide their contents. The dreamer may fear they have 'put all her eggs in one basket', thereby minimising their choices. A full basket indicates success and prosperity, while an empty basket signifies the approach of hard times or a lack of inspiration. If you dream about several baskets, it may reflect indecision over what to do next.

Baskets may appear as old-fashioned or traditional receptacles, hinting at the simplicity of country ways.

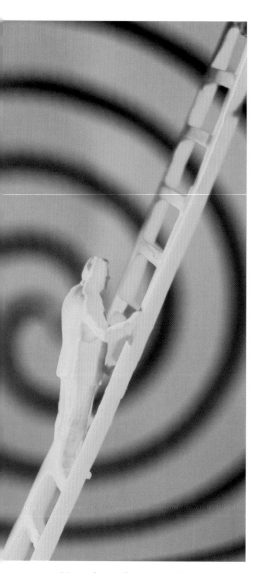

Ladders often reflect status in dreams, as they are used to climb up or down, to reach things that are normally unattainable.

Ladders are ancient symbols associated with spiritual advancement, the most famous being Jacob's wondrous dream about a ladder which reached towards heaven in the book of Genesis: 'And he dreamed there was a ladder set up on earth, the top of it reaching to heaven; and the angels of god were ascending and descending on it.' (Gen. 29.10).

Ladders are used to reach heights normally beyond us and a dream ladder may represent the dreamer's path through life, both now and in the future. You may dream about climbing the corporate ladder or perhaps the social ladder. Try to remember whether you reached the top in your dream, or whether something stopped you. Could you see what was at the top and, if so, were you keen to reach it? Reaching the top is an indication that you will achieve your goals. A dream about climbing down a ladder suggests that you are able to rethink your priorities, or that you are descending secure in the knowledge of a job well done. If you dream about a falling ladder, you must prepare for blows and disappointments, while either supporting or carrying a ladder suggests that you are able to help someone else with their ambitions and aspirations. To dream of becoming dizzy on a ladder implies that you have taken on too many responsibilities.

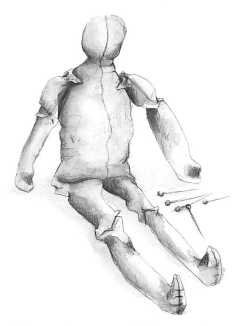

Toys are often simple reminders of childhood, with all the happiness or frustration that these memories entail. A dream about toys may suggest that the dreamer remains rather immature or childlike in a particular area of his life, or perhaps that he is acting childishly.

Dolls sometimes appear slightly creepy when left alone on a shelf and dream dolls often spring into life, appearing rather more menacing than their manufacturer intended. Anything enacted on a doll may reflect the dreamer's real wish to do the same thing to someone in real life.

Toys remind us of our childhood and of our children. The dreamer may simply want to reconnect with their inner child, returning to a time of certainties and protection. Dolls are often objects of intense affection, but alone on a shelf, untouched and unwanted, can appear strangely eerie. Dream dolls may come to life, perhaps representing aspects of the dreamer's personality. Alternatively, rather like voodoo dolls, they may symbolise someone that the dreamer dislikes.

Playing cards reflect the game of chance that is life, although the best dream sequence involving cards is undoubtedly in Lewis Carroll's *Alice in Wonderland*. Playing cards are endowed with particular symbolic meanings, but it may be sensible to regard them with the same refreshing attitude as Alice: `Why, they're only a pack of cards, after all. I needn't be afraid of them!'

Playing cards provide a diversion for both children and adults and, in dreams, represent the game of life. The dream may feature some sort of pun on the old adage of 'lucky in cards, unlucky in love'. If you dream of playing cards, you may shortly fall in love, although if you dream you are cheated, you should watch out for jealousy and treachery around you. If you are playing cards with a lover, you should question his or her intentions.

Each suit has a different meaning: diamonds are associated with money and careers; hearts with love; clubs with business and rewards from good deeds; and spades with troubles or obstacles. Aces signify fresh opportunities and new beginnings, and even the ace of spades may be a positive card as it implies that you have the power to put your troubles to right. The ace of clubs denotes financial security, the ace of diamonds implies that new ventures will begin shortly and the ace of hearts hints that romance is on the way.

The court cards all have specific meanings as well. The king of hearts represents a faithful lover; the king of diamonds means that you should beware of a powerful older man; the king of clubs stands for a loyal friend and the king of spades implies that there will be opposition to your plans. The queen of hearts relates to a loving woman or romantic news; the queen of diamonds indicates good news concerning property; the queen of spades means that a secret will be revealed; and the queen of clubs implies that although your career is fine, your love life needs attention. The jack of diamonds indicates that you will benefit from a small windfall or unexpected sum of money; the jack of hearts is a sign that a new love will enter your life; and the jack of spades represents a rival or opposition to something that is important.

Chapter 3

The Human Condition

'One of the characteristics of the dream is that nothing surprises us in it. With no regret, we agree to live in it with strangers, completely cut off from our habits and friends.'

Jean Cocteau 'Du rêve' from *La difficulté d'être*, 1947

The people who visit us in our dreams come from every area of our conscious and unconscious mind: family, lovers, friends, celebrities, someone we saw on the bus or complete strangers. They may represent archetypes (see page 63), or a facet of the dreamer's personality, or they may simply be appearing as themselves. Sometimes specific professionals appear, such as firefighters, refuse collectors or nurses, and their presence is probably intended to stress one aspect of the dreamer's psyche. Specific areas of the body can also be important and sometimes feature as puns to emphasise the message of the dream.

Childhood

Nostalgia plays an important part in the dreams of everyone, and dreams about one's childhood usually come into this category. Sometimes dreams about childhood occur during a particularly stressful phase of the dreamer's life, and are intended to remind the dreamer of a more innocent time when worries were almost non-existent.

The number of children in your dream may reflect your attitude to money: a large number of children means that you can expect financial rewards. More prosaically, if you are actually a parent to several children, you may be worried about how to finance them all!

Everyone dreams of their childhood at some point and these dreams may simply be nostalgic memories of lost youth. However, they may also reflect the dreamer's desire to escape the responsibilities and pressures of adult life, to recapture the days when there were very few demands on them. Such dreams might encourage us to adopt a more youthful attitude to life, to approach problems with a less serious outlook, and to seek the energy and optimism of the young. Dreams about children are generally seen as auspicious, especially in the fields of money and business; if you are worried about the health or behaviour of children in a dream, it may reflect your unease with the state of your own family, or possibly a concern about an aspect of your own childhood.

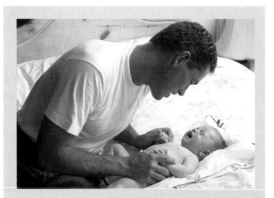

Baby dreams appear in many guises: expectant parents can be forgiven for dreaming about their new offspring and wondering just whose side of the family they will favour, but for the rest of the population, a dream baby does not necessarily represent a latent urge to become a parent.

Babies are important dream symbols, and herald new projects, creative potential or changes. However, consider the literal meaning first: do you feel like a helpless baby or feel the need for the comfort of a mother? Prospective parents often express their worries about their new responsibilities through their dreams. Shortly after the birth of my first child, I was troubled by a dream in which I had left her in a car, which was subsequently towed away by the traffic authorities and left in an enormous car park full of anonymous vehicles. The message here was perhaps more practical than symbolic,

but the dream was certainly an accurate reflection of my anxieties about how to cope with the demands of motherhood.

Dream babies often suffer dreadful fates: they get dropped, thrown away, lost or simply disappear, all symbolising lost opportunities or neglected talents. Dream babies may also appear with the wrong face, perhaps that of an older, uglier individual, or of some sort of magical creature. Such images represent fears that the new projects associated with the baby will be spoiled by outside interference. A baby that can walk unaided is symbolic of increasing independence by the dreamer. According to some theorists, a dream of a cradle indicates prosperity,

Twins often represent two sides of the same person, perhaps contrasting characteristics, or they may suggest that someone is two-faced. The zodiac sign of Gemini typically describes people born under that sign as lively and energetic, although this may be balanced by lethargy at times.

but if you see yourself rocking the cradle, it denotes illness or the problems that result from gossiping. A dream about having twins, implies you will have to work hard to keep up with your creations; they also represent two sides of a problem. Dream twins may also stand for someone born under the sign of Gemini, usually gregarious individuals of great energy.

Dreams of pregnancy indicate that something – an ambition, an idea for a lifestyle change, or a new project – is gestating and that you are bringing something to fruition. You have conceived some good ideas and are about to give birth to them; whether the birth is easy or not reflects how these ideas or plans will be received by the world around you.

The Divine Child is a very strong archetypal image, representing perfection, rebirth and innocence. It often appears in dreams of a spiritual nature. Such an image can signify the dreamer's potential for spiritual growth as it has enormous transforming and inspirational power, perhaps appearing to remind the dreamer that they have strayed from their original aspirations.

The image of a baby with its parents forms an almost divine group of three, (like the Holy Family).

Family

more likely an expression of frustration and a need to exert your independence. A parent may appear as a discredited figure – a drunk or a prostitute, for example – again reflecting a desire for independence. Everyone inherits some of their parents' characteristics, and for many the cry 'I'm turning into my mother', is the ultimate nightmare. However, dreams about parents provide the opportunity to reassess our relationships with them, and in turn, our relationships with our own children.

Family members usually appear in dreams as themselves, although they may be associated with the archetypes they stand for. So mothers may be seen as the universal earth mother archetype. Parents frequently appear in the dreams of adolescents; they are symbols of authority and most people dream of rebelling at some point in their lives. Dreams about killing your parents, whilst troubling, are probably not an augur of murderous intent, but

Mothers are always important figures in dreams.

Sibling rivalry is as old as mankind (remember Cain and Abel?), but equally, our siblings are our allies against our parents.

Dreams are one of our most basic outlets for the frustrations of family life, although the frequent appearance of your family in your dreams may suggest an over-dependence on them. The initial triangle of mother, father and baby is an important dream symbol, and is recreated again as two children struggle for their mother's attention. All children compete for the attention and love of their parents, and dreams about sibling rivalry that resurface in adult life are an expression of this basic insecurity. Some dream interpreters believe that dreams about brothers and sisters are a sign that the dreamer will enjoy a long life. If you see your brothers enjoying life, this may be a sign that good times are on the horizon for you too.

Dreams of grandparents signify an interest in your ancestry and roots. Their presence may remind you of your childhood and revive feelings of security and comfort. The appearance of a dead grandparent will probably be very reassuring, especially if they appear in a dream when you need guidance or advice.

Grandparents are often cited as a child's champion against their parents. To children, they appear wise, kind and loving, rarely imposing the same strict rules as the child's parents, so in dream symbolism they often represent wisdom and security.

101

Partners and lovers

Loving partners are often referred to as a 'dream couple' and that phrase is a rough indication that most relationships consist of more than simply gazing adoringly at each other.

Dream lovers are in many ways the ideal partner – behaving according to the whims of the dreamer. Of course, one cannot always predict who or what one will end up with… Most people dream of sex, and indeed during REM sleep both men and women experience a rush of blood and engorgement of their sexual organs. If you dream regularly about sex but rarely experience it in real life, it is probably time to find a loving partner. Dreams about lovers and lovemaking often fulfil Freud's theories about wish fulfilment: in dreams everyone can experience guilt-free pleasure with whomsoever they want.

Dreams about fixing cars or household gadgets sometimes reflect the state of your relationship or emphasise the dreamer's underlying disquiet. It may be a sign that you should examine your relationship to check that everything is working properly.

Real spouses and partners may be infrequent visitors in our dreams; dreamers often say that they felt their presence, or knew they were with them, but never actually saw them. This probably does not reflect an indifference on the part of the dreamer, merely the fact that the dream did not require the presence of such familiar people. (Although, if you are apart from your spouse, the meaning may alter somewhat.) A disturbing dream about a partner in an otherwise trouble-free relationship may be a warning to examine an issue that you have neglected or chosen to ignore.

Dreams about relationships may simply reflect your waking life, but look out for dreams about mending objects, such as broken cars or household items. They may hint that you should work on your relationship, and try to fix it before it breaks down.

Houses often symbolise the dreamer, so if you dream about fixing a dilapidated house, your self-esteem may need boosting. If you can boost your self-confidence it will undoubtedly improve relationships with those around you.

If you dream you are a part of an unhappy couple, compare the dream partnership with your own relationship to see whether the dream directs you to a particular aspect of your own relationship.

Emotions

Menacing eyes may frighten sleepers.

A dream about attacking a stranger may be an expression of pent-up aggression, or the stranger may symbolise an aspect of your own personality which you dislike.

We often wake from dreams with a greater sense of the powerful feelings we have experienced, than of the narrative, landscape or even the people of the dream. In many cases, the violent emotions of our dreams – fear, frustration, anger, envy – are expressions of feelings we repress during the day, perhaps out of politeness or feelings of inarticulacy. So, after a bad day at work, you may dream of attacking one of your colleagues, not necessarily because you wish them harm, but simply as a means of expressing your frustration. Anger, so often repressed during the day, explodes in dreams symbolically: dams of water burst, or buildings explode into flames. Frustration is often expressed through dreams about missing trains or buses, or about a long and fruitless search for a missing item. The dreamer should consider what the real problem is, especially if dreams of this sort recur.

Any dream about a never-ending task or where the dreamer feels impotent to control events around him suggests an underlying anxiety about some aspect of everyday life. For example, a dreamer may find himself helpless as dreadful things happen to friends or loved ones; or he may be faced with a desk piled high with an impossible amount of work.

There is nothing more frustrating than running for a train and arriving just as it moves out of the station: in dreams this is a classic anxiety dream as the dreamer struggles to reach his destination, only to be frustrated.

Alternatively, you may enjoy a classic wish-fulfilment dream about falling in love. Romantic dreams may reflect a dreamer's dissatisfaction with the state of his or her love life. Sometimes we dream about current relationships, which then become distorted by the dream, perhaps to help us explore the relationship from another perspective. ·Strangers may appear who represent a particular characteristic of your partner that the dream is encouraging you to examine more closely.

Optimistic or happy dreams often occur when we are at our most stressed and are the mind's way of compensating for the rigours of everyday life. In extreme circumstances, they can sustain hope during periods of bleak depression. Many survivors of the Nazi

Dreams about wedded bliss are not solely the preserve of romantic teenagers. Wedding dreams sometimes occur if the dreamer is on the brink of a new partnership, perhaps in business or sport, for example.

People who experience hardship in their waking life often experience dreams of blissful happiness as compensation for their miserable reality.

concentration camps of the Second World War reported that they experienced intensely happy dreams, filled with colour, images of their families, plentiful food and luxurious surroundings, all of which contrasted sharply with the conditions they lived in under the Third Reich. Equally, when humans have survived dangerous experiences, they often find they relive them through their dreams or nightmares. This was first noticeable on a large scale during and after the First World War, when many men returned home from war in the trenches. Unable or unwilling to tell their friends and family about the appalling conditions and sheer brutality of the war, many endured horrific dreams from which they woke sweating and shrieking. Having suppressed memories of their war experience during the daytime, they found them revived in their dreams, and this was the mind's way of dealing with the trauma. However, with time, the dreams declined in intensity as the former soldiers came to terms with their experiences (see pages 37–38).

Famous faces

Celebrities often make unlikely appearances in our dreams. Many people dream about people they admire either for their looks, such as pop stars or actors, or for their beliefs, such as politicians or writers. During the course of the 20th century a few famous faces acquired almost archetypal status as iconic representatives of their era. The names Elvis, Marilyn and Diana, for example, instantly conjure up individuals for whom no further explanation or epithet is necessary, and dreams about them probably owe as much to what they represent as to the individuals themselves. Other notable figures have come to embody particular virtues and vices: Adolf Hitler, for example is seen as the epitome of evil, while Winston

Celebrity dreams may be simple wish fulfilment, as the sleeper conjures up his heroes and heroines to entertain his dreams.

Churchill is regarded as the archetypal 'bulldog Brit' – a fine example of British stubbornness, defiant in the face of overwhelming odds. Royalty are common intruders into our dreams, possibly because they seem familiar. The Queen is apparently a popular dream figure, and may appear as a representative of power and authority (see page 58).

Some dreamers are appalled by the prospect of fame and may long to be left in peace.

Many people dream of achieving fame and fortune.

Dreams about famous people may simply reflect the dreamer's desire for a bit of glamour and excitement, or denote an ambition to follow in the footsteps of their heroes. The dreamer may crave recognition for achievements, or feel undervalued in some way. The appearance of famous people may simply underline the dreamer's feelings of inferiority in the company of such stellar individuals, although if the dream celebrity indulges in unexpectedly normal or even bad behaviour, the dream is clearly pointing out that they are no better than the dreamer.

The state we're in

Individual parts of the body are important symbols in dream interpretation, simply because they provide a wide range of metaphors for other parts of our lives. In more literal terms, many people have dreamed of illness before they have become evident or been diagnosed, and if you have recurring dreams about a particular complaint, it might be worth consulting your doctor. The ancient Greeks and Romans believed that dreams could be used to diagnose and cure illness, and even today the *British Medical Journal* has quoted recent research that dreams may 'reflect the presence of organic disease even when the patient is unaware of it.'

Most people have a dread of nudity in their waking lives, and the feeling of shame that exposure brings. In children,

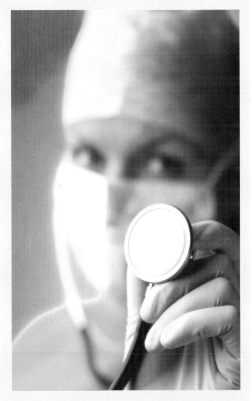

Some psychologists believe that a large part of some illnesses can be controlled by the mind and others cite evidence that suggests that patients dreamed about a particular problem before it was diagnosed by a doctor.

however, nudity is regarded as an innocent and natural, even beautiful, state. So nudity in dreams often occurs in scenarios that would shock us in our waking hours. Dreams of appearing nude

A dream about being naked as a child implies a wish to return to days of innocence, when the dreamer was unfettered by the restrictions of the adult world.

before friends or colleagues may reflect feelings of vulnerability, either of some aspect of our character or of something we do not want to come to light. If no one else in the dream notices the dreamer's nakedness, it indicates that fears of appearing foolish in front of others are unfounded. If others appear nude, the dream may indicate that the dreamer is able to see through the defences or lies of others. If the dreamer feels disgusted by the nudity of others in his dream, this may be an expression of disappointment in them, or reflect the dreamer's unwillingness to let others be themselves. If, however, the dreamer accepts the nakedness of those around him, he has probably shed outmoded beliefs and accepted others for what they are.

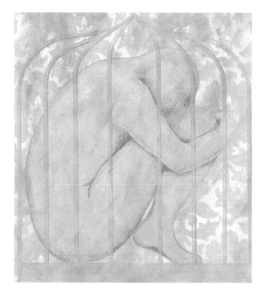

An image of shameful exposure.

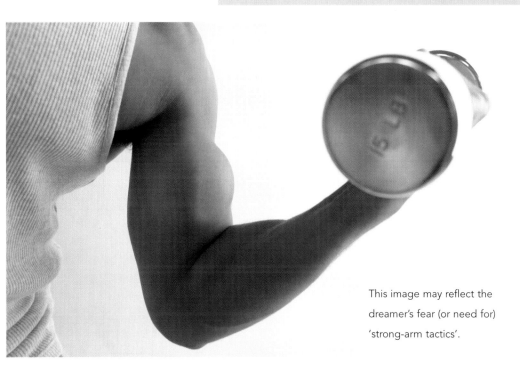

This image may reflect the dreamer's fear (or need for) 'strong-arm tactics'.

The rest of the body is an excellent source of dream imagery, particularly given the number of body-related metaphors in daily use. In general, the head and its features relate to spiritual or intellectual matters, whereas dreams of the torso or limbs are to do with physical concerns or instincts.

The heart, the traditional centre of our emotional lives and actual source of our life force, is naturally an important image. Phrases such as 'broken-hearted' or 'the heart of the matter' may feature in dreams, but it often represents love, either yours for

A symbol of a 'heart to heart'.

someone else, or the love that surrounds you. Blood is the life force within everyone – literally the life blood of the human race – and dreams about it relate to our physical and mental strength or general health. If you dream you are bleeding, you may be concerned about a loss of moral or physical strength; perhaps you simply need a holiday to recharge your batteries. If you dream of having blood on your hands, it is a powerful symbol of guilt: like Lady Macbeth, you may have trouble washing it off or covering your tracks. If you see other people bleeding, it may be a cry for help that you feel unable to answer.

A dream about bleeding may represent a fear that life is slipping away too fast.

A swollen head; is the dreamer over-confident?

The head is the centre of our intelligence and rational thought and the opposite of the heart in dream symbolism. Dreaming of a swollen head may be a warning about over-confidence, while a dream about beheading may hint that you need to 'keep your head' in a tricky situation. People are sometimes called 'hard-headed' and this may refer to a struggle between your head and your heart in an emotive situation.

Hair is an important part of self-image, so dreams of hair loss, or of going grey overnight may cause concern. A hair dream may encourage a dreamer to 'let his hair down' and take life less seriously.

Hair represents strength and vanity. We often refer to hair as our 'crowning glory' and, in the Bible, Samson lost his power along with his luxuriant locks. Dreams about going bald or cutting hair symbolises a loss of strength or protection, or possibly the renunciation of extravagance and worldliness where a dreamer wants to remove frivolity from his life and concentrate on those most important to him. A healthy beard represents vitality and a white one wisdom. If you dream that your hair suddenly turns white, this probably signifies a fear of encroaching age, or reflects some sort of stress in your waking life. The colour of hair may be significant: blond hair indicates love; brown or black hair indicates success in business; grey hair is indicative of approaching old age. Comparing a black hair with a white one means that you face a momentous decision. The associations of hair with virility and appearance mean that a dream of having a haircut may indicate a preoccupation with sexual performance.

A positive sign to look on the sunny side.

mythology an eye represented the all-seeing god. If your dream is peppered with eyes you probably feel a little paranoid. Eyes may reflect a dreamer's state of mind, so bleary or bloodshot eyes probably reflect a jaded spirit, whereas sparkling eyes are a sign of vitality and happiness. If you dream of being blind, consider whether there is something you are not seeing or refusing to face up to in your waking life; do you want to turn a 'blind eye' to a tricky situation? Ancient dream

Faces often become horribly transfigured, or one person may melt almost seamlessly into another in dreams, representing the dreamer's ambivalent feelings towards the two individuals. Phrases such as 'two-faced' or 'hard-faced' may also be significant. If the dream is about your own face, it probably reflects the Image you present to the world and how you 'face' others. Examine dream faces carefully for clues as to how others view you.

Eyes – the 'mirrors of the soul' – are often significant and in Egyptian

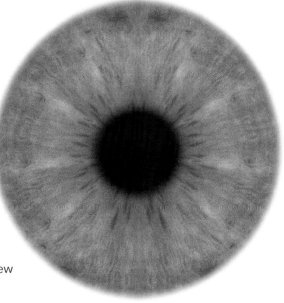

This eye reflects a fear of being 'eyeballed' or scrutinised too closely.

analysts believed that a dream about someone with bushy eyebrows promised success, while thin eyebrows indicated failure. If you dream your eyebrows fall out, your lover may not be faithful to you.

Ears remind you to listen out for good news and in many folktales magical words whispered into the ear bring about a magical transformation. If you dream you have become deaf and are cut off from the hearing world you must ask yourself why this has happened. It may indicate a desire to retreat from the hurly-burly of a frenetic lifestyle and find peace and quiet.

Noses may be signs of intuition as you 'sniff out' problems. If you dream that your nose is growing like Pinocchio's, your power and status in the world may be on the increase, and vice versa if it is shrinking. The dream may reflect Pinocchio's problem, however, and you may just be lying about something. Are you being nosey? Nosebleeds may signal a shock or a disaster.

Dreams of teeth falling out are very common and may signify the dreamer's need to return to a time when he had

Are your features being monitored?

The dreamer is advised to 'keep his nose clean' and stay out of trouble.

The dreamer's hands are tied, preventing him from addressing his problems.

no responsibilities, like a toothless child. Teeth fall out when we are children and again in great old age, and in dreams this may symbolise change; if you dream of losing your milk teeth you may dislike the idea of growing up and taking on new responsibilities. Alternatively, a dreamer may fear old age and the loss of power and control that comes with it. Traditionally, tooth loss in dreams means that you will acquire money.

If you dream about hands, consider their condition – are they clean, dirty, rough, wrinkled or smooth and manicured? Are you trying to 'wash your hands' of something, or do you fear being manhandled? Without our hands we are very limited in our capabilities, so dreams of injured hands may reflect fears of being unable to handle a situation or emotion. Arms represent protection and strength, as in a 'strong right arm'. Hands that are tied suggest that you are unable to make the changes you wish, while blood on your hands warns that you may suffer rejection. Shaking hands suggest that you need help from influential friends. You may dream of 'elbowing' your way through a crowd, which implies that you will overtake your rivals. A dream about a broken elbow, however, signifies business losses, while a pain in the elbow indicates obstacles and opposition.

Feet are another rich source of imagery, representing our ability to 'stand up' to people, or the fact that we might have

Shaking hand suggests friendship and agreement.

These men have no weapons and yet they are well-armed.

A baby's foot often provokes cries of amazement because it is so tiny, yet perfectly formed, and in dreams may symbolise that 'good things come in small packages'.

'put our foot in it'. Injured feet reflect an inability to move on or progress, or to 'stand on our own two feet', thus acting independently or supporting ourselves. Perhaps the dream is warning you to keep your 'feet on the ground' rather than become carried away with flights of fantasy. Aching feet traditionally represent family troubles, while stockinged feet stand for mysteries and secrets. Large feet are a sign of good health, while small feet indicate setbacks and an inability to progress. Burning feet are a surreal dream image and may symbolise jealousy, but hot feet are also a symptom of diabetes, so it may be wise to test for this possibility. If you dream of walking barefoot, you may have abandoned the restrictive constraints of everyday life, but it may also be a sign of impending poverty and ruin, perhaps appearing 'down at heel'. Everybody has a weakness – an 'Achilles heel' – and a dream about a painful heel may warn the dreamer to protect himself from attack.

Clothing

Many people find smart clothes rather daunting, whereas others revel the opportunity to appear well dressed. Clothes can mask our true selves and enable us to 'dress-up' as another person, so they can be useful disguises.

When clothes feature in your dreams, take note of their condition, as they depict the image you present to the world. Associated with status, gender, and occupation, the colour of your dream clothes may also be important (see pages 68–70). Tatty, ragged clothes suggest either that you fear impending poverty, or that you are unconcerned about your appearance and want to focus on more important spiritual or intellectual matters. If those around you are smartly dressed, consider your feelings in the dream – are you comfortable or do you feel out of place? Tight, restrictive clothing suggests that the dreamer feels inhibited by his public or professional life. Smart clothes suggest a preoccupation with the finer things in life and a concern to present the right image to the world. But do your clothes feel restrictive or hide the real you? If your dream clothes are a uniform of some sort, they may indicate a feeling that your individualism is being cloaked or hidden, indicating a desire to break free from the conformity around you. Uniforms are usually related to institutions and figures of authority, so the dreamer may feel overwhelmed by the authority figures in his life.

Individual items of clothing may also have their own symbolism in dreams. Hats, crowns and headdresses are important as they often denote power and status. Dreams about being crowned reflect the dreamer's desire for recognition and status, and the alternative – losing a crown or hat – probably hints at anxieties about losing such status. Crowns generally suggest an improvement in the dreamer's circumstances, while a dream about crowning a friend indicates that you are a generous-hearted person. Hats, which protect the head, are regarded as a good omen in the dreams of business people who obviously need to 'keep their heads' in their work environment.

A hard hat is protective and in dreams may symbolise the dreamer's need to protect himself from others, or from a perceived mental onslaught

Coats protect the wearer against the elements, so a dirty or torn coat suggests that the dreamer will suffer some sort of material loss; losing a coat implies that you will have to recover losses. If you dream of wearing someone else's coat, you will ask a friend for support and they will stand by you. Cloaks often represent concealment and secrecy and cloaked figures in dreams may appear sinister or simply mysterious; cloaks can hide both good and bad things, so if you are suspicious of what is behind a cloak, confront the wearer and you may be surprised.

A dream cloak may simply be a pun reflecting what the dreamer is cloaked in. Cloaks are all-enveloping and may symbolise love and protection: perhaps the dreamer feels smothered by their dream cloak, or perhaps it is too small and does not offer enough protection.

Neckties indicate formality and the ties of work.

Collars and ties are symbolic of the modern workplace for many men, but collars have an ancient significance, and can stand for either nobility or slavery, depending on the style of the item. Slaves in Roman times and later were restrained with iron collars and chains, while the high collars of 19th century dress, for example, were a sign of money and nobility. Neckties are a very masculine image and, in Freudian interpretation, a woman's dream about wearing a tie would suggest competitive envy. If a man dreams he is wearing a dress, it is probably not latent

The small items we are all obliged to carry around with us – handbags, wallets, purses and credit cards – are often referred to as part of our 'life-support systems'. In dreams, as in life, we feel lost without them and a dream about searching for them reflects anxiety and insecurity.

transvestitism coming to the fore, but possibly a cue to get in touch with his feminine side and the more caring aspects of his nature.

Accessories such as handbags, wallets or purses are very personal items which in dreams may reflect concerns about individuality or identity. Used to carry money, vital personal information and small photos of loved ones, a lost purse or wallet provokes very real anxiety, which, in a dream context, reflects feelings of insecurity; you may feel 'lost' without it and miss the perceived support of all those credit cards and telephone numbers. In Freudian terminology, a purse symbolises the womb.

At a young age, many small boys are fascinated by their mother's clothes and make-up, and in dreams this simply reflects their love for their mother. A man's dream about wearing a dress may simply reflect the dreamer's desire to share more of his mother's characteristics.

Activities

Washing represents the dreamer's need to cleanse himself of a problem or feelings. Shakespeare probably used the image to best symbolic effect when he gave the line 'What! Will these hands ne'er be clean?' to the murderous and increasingly mad Lady Macbeth, whose guilt about the untimely demise of several royals began to plague her.

Humdrum activities, such as sleeping, eating or washing, feature as much in our dreams as in our daily lives. Such dreams often incorporate the trivia of the day and are sometimes the mind's way of filing events, but they can become interesting if something untoward or completely bizarre happens. Rooms may be familiar, but the furniture may be wrong, appliances may have grown or shrunk in size, total strangers may appear to live in your house – all of these examples should encourage the dreamer to examine his home life from a slightly different perspective.

Domestic activities often reflect our relationships with our families. Cooking and serving food, for example, may symbolise a wish to influence others or make them dependent. Washing ourselves is about cleansing our spirits – perhaps washing away shame, while

Cooking and sharing food is a method of showing that you love those around you and want to look after them. In dreams cooking is also associated with influence and, to a lesser extent, power.

A dream about washing a child may reflect the great love of a parent for his offspring – the water represents the dreamer's love that he is pouring over the baby..

dreams of bathing your children may represent your need to look at your aspirations for the future and polish or increase your ambitions. Cleaning the house is another activity full of potential symbolism. Dream houses embody the dreamer, so cleaning it reflects a desire to simplify or clarify aspects of your life or to try to understand feelings that have been troubling you. Take note of which room you are cleaning; if you are in the cellar, you may be trying to unearth hidden memories of long-forgotten incidents or grudges, while the dust in a dream attic is stifling your urges to be more cerebral or spiritual.

Eating is an important aspect of our daily lives and an interesting source of dream metaphors. Freud noted that the mouth was the first erogenous zone discovered by children, and eating has always been linked to sex; they are both sensual activities. If, in your dreams, you are hungry or thirsty, it may be that real physical needs are inserting themselves into your dream. However, it may also express the need for greater affection or intellectual nourishment. Meals are a social ritual and food can represent spiritual as well as physical sustenance in dreams. If you not be entirely normal; indeed the dreamer may find themselves eating completely unsuitable objects, perhaps even another person. If you find you have become a dream cannibal, this act, not surprisingly, stands for hostility towards the person you are eating; you may be eating up an aspect of your own character which you despise. If you dream you are being consumed, are you 'eaten up' by a problem? Or perhaps you feel your personality itself is being devoured by forces beyond your control?

Food can symbolize intellectual nourishment, so sharing a meal in a dream may be about the dissemination of ideas and opinions.

dream of enjoying a meal with someone, it may reflect a desire to get closer to them, perhaps to enjoy a physical relationship. If the dream is about eating with others, it could symbolise the sharing of ideas.

The food consumed in a dream may

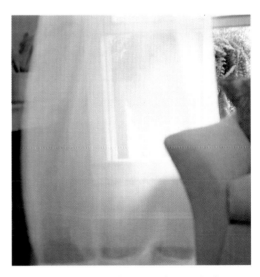

If you dream you are cleaning a house, look at the rooms you are tidying as they represent the aspect of your personality that needs attention.

Occupations

Anyone who actually has defective vision may simply dream about a visit to the optician as a factual dream. However, peer beneath the surface and consider whether the dream is trying to tell you that you are being 'short-sighted' about a problem, or if you need to confront someone eyeball to eyeball.

Occupations, either one's own or those of others, are common dream themes. Once again, puns and metaphors may be important: a dream about a visit to the optician may hint that you are being short-sighted about a problem. A dream about working in a huge call centre with rows of identical computers and desks reflects anxieties about loss of identity and individualism, while dreams about trying to sell things to uninterested customers suggest that your powers of communication need improvement.

Uniforms add both status and definition to an individual; it is obvious how they are employed and the uniform often commands the respect of onlookers. The most obvious examples are policemen or soldiers, firefighters or medical professionals. Some people, however, fear authority and associate uniforms with a loss of identity and freedom. Other professional figures may appear in dreams, from angels to wizards, and beggars to waiters, and each enjoys its own symbolism, which may also be personal to the dreamer.

Soldiers can be either aggressive killers or heroic defenders, depending upon which end of their gun is facing you. So, if you dream you are a soldier, consider whether your aggressive or protective instincts are uppermost. Do you simply want someone to fight your battles for you? The appearance of

Large offices with their identical workstations of grey computers can be soul-destroying places, and a dream about working in one may reflect a feeling of lost identity or of blending unnoticed into the background.

Policemen are obvious authority figures, who instil fear and loathing, or respect and relief, depending on one's circumstances. Sometimes they appear as distorted figures, reflecting puns such as 'the long arm of the law'.

soldiers veers between the smart uniformed formality of the parade ground and the camouflaged and bloodied combat veteran: Jane Austen remarked in *Pride and Prejudice* that a 'young man wanted only regimentals to make him completely charming', so for many, a gallant dream soldier may simply be part of a harmless fantasy. The dreamer may feel that his life needs a touch of military discipline, although dreams of being part of a large army may reflect fears about loss of freedom and individuality.

A less comfortable dream about a battle probably reflects unresolved conflicts in the dreamer's life. The dreamer may simply be a bystander or perhaps a peacemaker; or if the

Doctors can appear as god-like figures with the power of life or death over their patients. Dreams about being a doctor imply that the dreamer wants to help others.

dreamer is involved it may indicate that trouble is on the horizon and he may be outnumbered.

Doctors and nurses are often the focus of our attention when we are at our most vulnerable and needy. Thus

127

Professional soldiers enjoy almost universal respect because they dedicate their lives to defending their country, often at the expense of their own life. They are often regarded as heroes and a dream about being a soldier may be wish fulfilment in this respect. A dream battle may reflect the dreamer's internal conflict over some sort of dilemma.

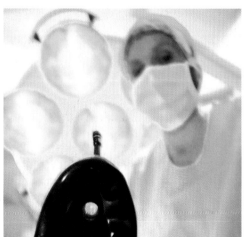

If you dream you are undergoing an operation, it may be a reflection of your underlying fears about your own health. A dream about operating on someone else may symbolise latent feelings of aggression towards them, as you want to cut up part of them.

they are endowed with heroic and healing qualities. If you dream that you are being treated by a doctor, you are probably aware that you have a spiritual or physical problem; try to see which area of your body is treated in the dream, as this may have additional significance. If you dream you are undergoing an operation, this may reflect a subconscious realisation that something is wrong in your life, perhaps with a relationship, and must be cut out. If you dream you are the surgeon, it is an expression of your ability to face problems and deal with them effectively.

A dream about being a butcher may express hidden feelings of aggression: butchering meat is a very physical job, involving chopping and slicing. In dreams you may find that it is not just meat that you cut up.

Butchers are associated with both slaughter and nourishment, so their dream symbolism will depend on the context. Some sources suggest that if you dream of a butcher slaughtering an animal, illness will affect a member of your family, while watching a butcher at work hints that you will receive a bad reference (this may be a pun about your character being 'butchered'). Dreaming about meat implies carnal knowledge or instincts.

Postmen are to do with communication and messages, so the appearance of one indicates that news is on its way. Consider your reaction when you see the postman – do you welcome his arrival or dread hearing bad news? Letters themselves may suggest that long-distance concerns may become important to you, or remind you of the need to get in touch with long-lost friends or relatives. If you dream you are delivering letters, this may represent a pent-up need to communicate more frequently with friends; it may also characterise a shy dreamer, who wants to socialise but is too timid to do it face-to-face.

Postmen or mailmen are messengers and their appearance in a dream may remind the dreamer of the need to be more open with those around him, or alternatively, to get in touch with long-lost friends or relatives.

Dream rubbish is often surprising; the dreamer may find that he or she has thrown out valuable possessions and the message inherent in this type of dream is that he or she should pay less attention to material wealth.

If a priest appears in your dream, it may be a reflection of your need to confess something; perhaps you harbour a dark secret which you feel unable to talk about with friends or relatives.

Refuse collectors have a thankless job, but without their work the clean streets that we take for granted would be clogged with rubbish. A dream about a refuse collector may imply that you need to 'clean up your act', perhaps be more honest in your dealings with those around you. It may remind you to streamline your life, to pare down your emotional commitments to those who are truly vital to your well-being. Chimney sweeps share similar associations, although traditionally they are regarded as extremely lucky, especially at weddings. Their links to fire denote passion, which is helpful in a successful marriage.

Religious figures, such as priests and nuns, usually relate to the spiritual side of life, although because they are associated with complex issues that we never entirely understand, they may have slightly sinister implications. The vision of the 'mad monk', a dark hooded figure, can be a frightening dream image with uncomfortable overtones and may refer to a secretive person. Monks are often silent contemplative figures, however, and may indicate calm and inner peace. If you dream of an abbot or abbess, you

Angels embody the best characteristics of humans and are touched with divinity. The dreamer may wish that their lifestyle is more angelic and peaceful.

may need to submit to an authority figure, although a friendly abbess indicates support and guidance. Many people regard members of the clergy as father figures (which is how they are often addressed) and if they feature in a dream it may reflect the dreamer's need to seek advice. Any of these figures may embody a dreamer's spiritual aspirations.

Angels are heavenly messengers and it is sensible to listen to what they have to say if one appears in your dreams. They represent spiritual guidance and protection, but may also warn against immoral or unkind behaviour.

A dream about a beggar may reflect the dreamer's own neediness: he may feel excluded, spiritually impoverished and desperate for help. The dreamer may learn from the dream beggar to recognise his own good fortune; if he gives money to the beggar it is a sign of good luck, whereas refusing is a bad omen.

Burglars or intruders are usually threatening figures, out to invade our homes and rob us of our possessions. Their

A dream about giving away money is a sign of generosity and may hint that prosperity is on the way. It might also indicate a lack of interest in material possessions.

appearance in dreams might be a warning to protect ourselves better. They may also be an expression of the dreamer's 'shadow', the part of our character we keep hidden. You may try to repel the burglar in your dream, only to find that he suddenly becomes friendly: this insinuates that there is a part of your subconscious that you need to address.

Fairies often endow humans with magical power in dreams and may represent wishes which haven't come true.

Burglars are sinister figures who threaten us in our homes where we usually feel most secure. A dream about a burglary may reflect basic feelings of insecurity, or the dreamer may feel that an aspect of his life or character is threatened.

Mythical or magical figures – fairies elves, goblins, witches, wizards, for example – appear in the mythology and legends of every culture. Fairies traditionally grant wishes, or sprinkle mortals with dust to give them magical qualities. In dreams they may represent unfulfilled childhood wishes. Witches and wizards have recently acquired an excellent new public relations guru in the form of J K Rowling and her creation, Harry Potter, so witches and wizards may now appear in dreams as more humourous, equally magical, but less threatening characters than in earlier years. Giants may stand for a person or object that appears to tower over the dreamer in an intimidating way, and is perceived as an obstacle. They may also hark back to the dreamer's childhood, when all adults seemed like giants, sometimes benign and at other times forbidding.

Children often regard witches as scary characters, but literature and folklore abound with examples of good witches, who use their magical powers to help people. Witches and other supernatural figures appear in children's dreams as manifestations of their unspoken fears.

Chapter 4

Journeys and Milestones

'The interpretation of dreams is the royal road to a knowledge of the unconscious activities of the mind.'

Sigmund Freud,
The Interpretation of Dreams (1909)

The significance of milestones such as births, deaths and marriages cannot be underestimated – they are quite simply what make individuals who they are, marking their passage through time. Any decisions relating to these events, therefore, are likely to be reflected in our dreams. The occasions themselves, the ceremony and administration associated with them or any doubts about the people involved, may also appear in dreams, either in the form of wish fulfilment or, given the potential stress involved, as anxiety dreams.

Many people who have undergone a major life-changing event, such as birth, bereavement or marriage may find their dreams full of comforting images, perhaps of their childhood, or of familiar faces and favourite haunts. The unconscious mind is helping the dreamer to adapt to the changes in life by providing reassuring scenarios to help the dreamer feel inwardly secure during times of change.

Pregnancy is as old as history, but first-time mothers are often overwhelmed by feelings of astonishment and responsibility for the new life inside them. Dreams about pregnancy are often related to hopes for new projects or adventures in your life.

Birth

Dreams about birth occur among both men and women and, unless the dreamer is actually pregnant, they usually represent the dreamer's attitude to a new project or phase in their life. Pregnant women often dream about the act of giving birth, particularly first-time mothers who may be facing the fear of the unknown. If you dream you are present at a birth, as a father or helper, this symbolises your encouragement and support for someone else's ideas.

Psychologists disagree about whether or not we remember anything of our own birth experience, but if you dream you are being born, say by emerging from a long tunnel or crawling out of a small hole, remember that this past experience has very little bearing on the current state of your life. Another school of thought believes that such dreams reflect the dreamer's desire for rebirth, perhaps a chance to live life again without the mistakes of the past – a theme that becomes more meaningful with increasing age.

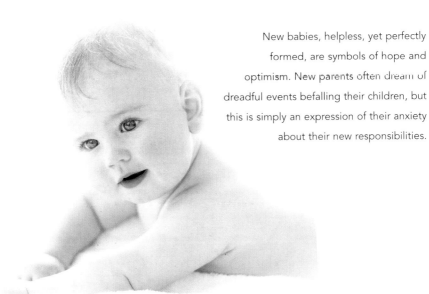

New babies, helpless, yet perfectly formed, are symbols of hope and optimism. New parents often dream of dreadful events befalling their children, but this is simply an expression of their anxiety about their new responsibilities.

Death

Dreams about death are often disturbing, leaving the dreamer feeling either guilty or worried, depending on the events of the dream. Primarily, one is scared of having experienced a precognitive dream. Many people report dreams in which a friend or relative has appeared and said goodbye to them, only to discover on waking that that person really died during the night. Death dreams are sometimes followed by bad news from the individuals concerned, and can be a means of preparing individuals for the death of someone close to them. Equally, dreams about the recently-dead often help dreamers to grieve and to accept their loss. The dreamer may see their loved one in the past when they were happy together, or in a completely new and obviously pleasant place. Dreams of this nature usually leave the bereaved dreamer feeling reassured and comforted.

Dreams about funerals can be pretty depressing, perhaps even worrying if you dream about the funeral of someone close to you.

Dreams about murdering colleagues, friends or relatives are often subconscious expressions of aggression which cannot be uttered during the day.

In more general terms dreams in which death is a feature signify closure, or the end of a phase or event in the dreamer's life. The dream may enable the dreamer to realise that all things must come to an end and that death is often a release, enabling the dreamer to move on to new opportunities. Death dreams are more likely to be about change than mortality.

Death dreams can also be cathartic; a dreamer may dream about killing an especially obnoxious acquaintance or colleague, and this may help them to face them during their waking hours.

The unconscious has allowed the dreamer to express the hostility they have to repress during their waking hours. The person killed in your dream may represent an aspect of your personality that you wish to 'kill off'; this is more likely if the dead person is not someone you recognise. Dreams about killing people of whom you are fond are also normal, but may leave a dreamer feeling worried by the strength of feelings of which he may not have been conscious. This kind of dream probably enables a dreamer to appreciate the finer qualities of the other person on waking, however.

Sometimes one may dream of one's own funeral – you may even cry at the thought of your own death. A dream of this nature reflects fears of mortality.

Graveyards are places of burial; in dreams they may symbolise the need to bury an aspect of the dreamer's life.

Dreams about one's own death and funeral have an element of narcissism about them, as many people are curious about how their families and friends would react to their demise. A dream about one's own death may simply be an exercise in curiosity to examine how the world would cope without him or her. If your dream includes large numbers of people weeping at the prospect of your demise, it may be comforting and perhaps compensate for feelings of neglect that you experience during the day. More seriously, a dream about one's own death may signify fear and a wish to retreat from the problems of life. A dream about one's own burial may express the dreamer's wish to bury an aspect of his or her life or personality; perhaps there are objects in the coffin that point to exactly what the dreamer wishes to leave behind. Or the dreamer may wish to return to the comfort of the womb. A dream of this type may also reflect a morbid fear of being buried alive, or more prosaically, heavy bedclothes may simply be piled on top of the dreamer.

If you dream of crying and grieving, try to remember what
you are mourning—is it someone dear to you, or perhaps the
loss of youth or innocence?

Tombs of the 16th and 17th centuries often feature skulls, bones and whole skeletons, *memento mori* symbolising the eventual fate of every living thing.

Symbols of mortality and death often provoke fear and an accompanying shiver down the back of the spine. They were common images in religious paintings and churches during the Middle Ages, intended to remind people of their mortality and the need to repent their sins. Such *memento mori* include skulls, skeletons, scythes, the 'grim reaper', hourglasses and tombstones. Dreams about graves or cemeteries are rarely signs of impending death, but are more likely to reflect the dreamer's need to bury a relationship or problem. They are places where we come to terms with death and are also considered to be an indication of recovery from illness or an unfortunate situation. Similarly, graves are a sign that you should put the past behind you and move on.

In general, dreams about death reflect an underlying need to accept our fate, that the circumstances of life are constantly changing, and the fact that eventually we will all die. They may remind us to make the most of our lives and to live to our full potential.

Ceremonies

Formal ceremonies are important markers of our passage through life, tangible reminders of life's transience and mutability. Every culture in the world has used rituals and festivals to mark important stages such as birth, puberty, marriage, parenthood and finally death, as well as ceremonies to celebrate recurrent events such as spring, harvest and the winter solstice. These days, the more elemental worries about whether the harvest would be plentiful enough to feed everyone through the winter have given way to consumer commercialism over the cost of gifts which we now exchange at many ceremonies, or how to cope with the catering for a wedding buffet. Human beings have always suffered from stress, and although the reasons for it change, worries are still reflected in our dreams.

In many primitive societies, dreams and dream interpretation formed an important part of rituals and festivals.

Flamboyant weddings do not just happen, but are the result of many weeks of planning. Weddings are also a very public display of affection and, to some extent, status. A dream wedding may represent the stress and anxiety involved in the preparation, or a partnership of some sort.

Giving and receiving is a symbol of social relationships, so in dreams gifts and presents represent the esteem in which we are held by others.

A christening is an important event in the life of a young baby and the chance for its family to introduce him or her formally to the wider world. Baptism is a form of ritual initiation and acceptance, and a dream baptism may suggest that the dreamer feels a need for recognition and perhaps the blessing of his or her peers and family for aspects of his behaviour or life. It may also symbolise new beginnings and the chance to start again, free from old problems and difficulties. If you dream you are a godparent to a baby, this may stand for your support of a new project or enterprise; if you are the person being baptised, however, it represents a desire to wash away present difficulties and begin a new life.

Christenings share the symbolism associated with newborn babies, but they incorporate an added religious dimension whereby someone is welcomed by friends and family.

Dreams about weddings are heavily dependent on the dreamer's personal circumstances, but may be wish fulfilment if the dreamer longs to marry. Fundamentally, marriage is about the union of two people, so in dreams it may reflect a business partnership or even just a sporting partner. Wedding dreams often become surreal, with either partner turning into the wrong person, disasters befalling the guests or the church turning into a ship.

Interestingly, these are exactly the sort of anxiety dreams encountered by many happy couples-to-be! Nineteenth-century dream interpreters, who often applied a system of opposite meanings to dream symbolism, believed that wedding dreams hinted at bad luck and bitterness to come. If a woman dreams that something prevents her wedding, it reflects her apprehension at the prospect of some sort of union, but not necessarily a partnership as serious as marriage. It could be about work or something as insignificant as a tennis partner, for example.

Parties which go wrong inflict a very public humiliation on the host or hostess and in dreams represent fears that the dreamer is not accepted by his or her peers.

Many people dream about marrying a 'fantasy' partner, but more comical sometimes is a dream about marrying someone or something who is completely inappropriate. This type of dream may reflect apprehension about an actual wedding or perhaps concerns about another sort of partnership.

145

If you frequently dream about gracing large parties with your witty presence, the dream may be compensating for a rather emptier social life and may be a hint that you need to get out more.

Celebrations are an important aspect of many formal events and dreams of feasts and banquets often relate to the dreamer's place in public life. If you dream of organising a great banquet to be enjoyed by hundreds of your closest friends, you may be wanting to show off your talents to a wider audience. Perhaps the dreamer is really a shy person and wishes he or she was more of an extrovert. A dream about attending a large party is about the dreamer's place in society; parties are convivial and fun, so a crowded party implies that the dreamer enjoys popularity in a wide circle of friends. If you dream you arrive at a dismal empty party, this probably reflects feelings of loneliness. A dream about overindulgence, either eating too much or becoming drunk, may be a hint for you to lessen demands on family and friends.

A busy person caught up in a social whirl may sometimes long for solitude and in a kind of perverse way, dream almost longingly of loneliness and the comparative peace of that state.

Journeys

Dream journeys often reflect the dreamer's passage through life, his movement from one great milestone to another, or simply his passage from one challenge to the next. Life is constantly on the move and outgoing individuals should try to embrace the opportunities offered by a change of circumstance. Those who do not will remain in a rut, stagnating and possibly frustrated. Of course, everyone reacts differently to change and some people are slow to accept the need for it. Our dreams often help us to resolve difficulties of this nature, allowing the mind time to assess situations that may eventually lead to a fulfilled and happy life.

Challenges in life are usually stimulating and exciting, although at times they may threaten to overwhelm us.

Before embarking on any journey, we assess the distance involved, the mode of transport, the destination and the direction. Consider all these factors when assessing a dream journey. The destination represents your goal or ambition and the journey itself the means of achieving it. Travellers are often forced to relinquish direct control

A person who is frustrated in his daily life may dream of adventures and excitement.

A journey along a clear, straight road is trouble-free and uncomplicated, perhaps reflecting the dreamer's progress through life.

over their progress and are slowed down by circumstances beyond them: trains are delayed, roadworks or road accidents impede car journeys and these are a manifestation of the dreamer's anxiety over the fear of failure.

If we regard life as a journey, then the path upon which we travel is highly significant. Your dream road may be straight and smooth, or sometimes rocky and covered with obstacles. Perhaps you are travelling through life in a boat along a river. If you encounter a difficult route, you must question whether obstacles are self-imposed or whether they can be surmounted. Sometimes, they provide a welcome break and a chance to sit back and enjoy the scenery; at other times they are simply frustrating impediments to progress. You may feel uncertain about your journey and unsure whether it is a good idea; these feelings probably reflect confusion about taking on a new job or leaving home.

A dream about a train journey may reflect the dreamer's progress through life. Trains travelling fast into tunnels, however, are often regarded as a sexual symbol.

Any scenery along the route often symbolises the state of the dreamer's inner life. A dream about travelling endlessly across an arid desert, for example, suggests a rather bare, even empty soul in need of refreshment (see page 205) There are many metaphors associated with travelling which reflect life's journey: we become 'sidetracked', reach a 'dead end' or find that progress is 'uphill work'. The more adventurous may go 'off the beaten track,' while others have no problems and find that it is 'plain sailing.'

A river journey may symbolise the dreamer's emotional life.

Arid, sandy and scorchingly hot, dream deserts are often places of emotional emptiness

149

A dream about travelling in an easterly direction towards the rising sun implies an optimistic outlook as the dreamer faces the new day and new challenges ahead.

Dreams in which darkness obscures the landscape are often unsettling or frightening. If a child experiences a dream like this, it may simply represent their fears of the dark.

The direction of a journey is also of significance. Travelling east towards the rising sun, for example, implies optimism and courage. The journey may take place in the dark, but the dreamer is encouraged by the prospect of illumination towards the end of the expedition. Travelling west, in the direction of the setting sun, implies perhaps a metaphorical journey towards maturity or even death. More complicated directions are also critical. Fears of becoming lost on a dream journey are related to an anxiety about losing one's identity or purpose in life. Maps that appear may not be conventional, perhaps bearing only one word or picture rather than a route. They are symbols of self-knowledge and might help you discover something new about yourself; the same may be true of road signs.

Crossroads and other road junctions obviously represent decisions that must be made about life's journey. Mazes or labyrinths are more confusing and reflect a crisis in life – the dreamer literally has no idea which way to go. If you are faced with a choice between taking the high road or the low road, this means that you have to choose between an idealistic solution and a more selfish one. If you find yourself careering downhill, out of control but with a feeling of exhilaration, you probably want to leave the confines of your structured journey through life and find a more exciting means of travel. Conversely, struggling up a steep hill implies that you are asking too much of yourself and perhaps need to consider a different path in life.

Many dream journeys do not feature destinations at all; the important thing is the journey itself and what the dreamer experiences on the way. Many journeys feature dead ends, or disappointing destinations and are something of an anti-climax; if you are trying to understand a dream of this nature, concentrate on the journey itself as the destination may well be superfluous to the message of the dream. Another common theme is missing a train or bus, symbolising a fear of missed opportunities (see also page 162).

We are propelled on journeys by various different means: on foot, by bicycle, on horseback, in a plane, train or car or in a boat. The means of travel

If you reach a crossroads when on a journey, you must decided which way to go, and similarly, a dream about a crossroads may be a pun which represents the dreamer's need to make a decision.

The appearance of a steep hill may represent some sort of obstacle in the dreamer's life which must be surmounted before he can progress.

151

Walking is the ultimate form of self-sufficient transport and as a dream symbol represents self-reliance and independence. Walking a tightrope, however, is about balance in one's life, perhaps indicating the stresses between work and home.

is important as it reflects the dreamer's self-image and his feelings about the degree of control he has over his future. The pace of travel is also interesting simply because it symbolises the speed with which the dreamer can attain his destination or ambitions.

A dream about a long journey on foot suggests that the dreamer is confident about his abilities to propel himself along the path of life without any outside help, keen to embrace the challenges thrown up by the open road. Walking, running or swimming all suggest self-sufficiency and the fact that the dreamer feels perfectly in control of his or her destiny. The same is true, to an extent, of cycling, as the dreamer or rider drives himself with his own power. If you dream you are carrying a load such as a backpack, consider whether you feel over-burdened by it, as it may represent a feeling that you are 'carrying' a colleague at work, for example.

If you dream you are riding an animal, be aware that it might express an aspect of your personality (see page 229), which may be driving you forward, particularly if the animal seems too powerful for you to control. Horses may symbolise controlled strength as the rider submits the power of the animal to his domination, and some dream interpreters believe that dreams about riding a horse represent sexual intercourse.

If you dream you are travelling in a vehicle, consider who is driving. If you are driving a car, you are clearly in charge of where you are going, and this represents confidence and independence on the part of the dreamer. If someone else is driving, think about whether you are 'being

Riders harness the power of the horse and use it for their own ends. In dreams, this kind of control may be the wish of someone who feels that they have little influence over the progress of their life.

In dreams about a car journey, try to remember who was driving the car and if you were happy about the way it was being driven as this reflects the feelings of control you have over your life.

taken for a ride' and whether or not you are comfortable to be under the control of another person. Do you like the way they drive, or are they driving too fast and furiously for you to feel safe? If you recognise the driver of the car, are you considering some sort of close relationship with them? Perhaps there is no driver and the car is simply careering along out of control; if this is the case, there is probably an area of your life that you feel powerless to control and you should try to regain the upper hand.

Dream cars are sometimes representations of the dreamer and reflect his or her self-esteem. An old, run-down car obviously needs some care and attention.

Look at the condition of the vehicle, as it embodies a dreamer's personality. If you dream you are driving a rusty old banger, this suggests that you have a poor self-image; by contrast a dream about driving a powerful sports car implies supreme confidence, perhaps even over-confidence. Colour may be important here as it reflects how you want the world to see you. If the car breaks down, think about whether you are putting yourself under undue strain in your waking life; perhaps you need to pamper yourself with a service? Mechanical failure of a dream car usually relates to an emotional crisis in the dreamer's life; a breakdown on a deserted road in the middle of nowhere reflects the dreamer's feelings of being unloved with no one to turn to for help. A car

A dream about a mechanical breakdown may be an anxiety dream about the dreamer's ability to reach a real destination, or it may represent some sort of emotional crisis, as the dreamer himself, represented by the car, actually has a breakdown.

A CAR DREAM

A woman dreamed that her husband's car was parked among other cars, in a narrow lane, on a snowy day. It was just after Christmas and the snow was old and dirty. She saw herself nearby and had to stand back as a bright blue 4x4 jeep drove past too fast and too close to her husband's car. The jeep seemed deliberately to veer close to the car and scratched its bodywork. The dreamer was cross and shook her fist at the jeep, which stopped. An ugly old woman looked out and told her that she should have moved the car, and then drove off up a hill without giving her insurance details. The dreamer shouted that she would catch her anyway from the number plate, 'T T T T T.'

Interpretation: the old snow symbolised a longstanding feeling of remoteness in the dreamer's relationship with her husband. The husband's car represented her husband; the fast jeep, the attentions of other people who seemed threatening, (although once the dreamer saw the driver, she realised they were not). The dreamer surprised herself with her feelings of protectiveness towards the car.

crash represents confrontation or disagreement; if the dreamer comes off worst, it may represent a desire to punish him or herself for something.

Dreams about driving vehicles you are unaccustomed to, such as aeroplanes, trains or coaches might hark back to childhood ambitions. Alternatively, these dreams may be offering a different perspective on your life.

A flight in a plane enables the dreamer to gain an overview of the landscape (or life) ahead of him and to prepare for obstacles or problems in the future. It may be worth remembering that cars and ships are traditionally referred to as she, so in men's dreams such vehicles may represent any of the dreamer's female relations. Conversely, motorbikes are regarded as masculine symbols, signs of a man's virility and power.

This surreal dream image suggests that the dreamer wants to exert more control over the direction of his life. He is astride the plane (which could be a phallic symbol) and can therefore dominate how it flies. The parcel represents his past life – he wants to move on to pastures new, but does not want to forget earlier events in his life.

If you dream about driving a bus or train, you are willing to assume control over the journeys of others and this kind of dream may reflect a desire for greater responsibility at work. A train journey propels you along a preordained track from which there is no escape, and dreams may focus on metaphors about being derailed, getting back on the right track or being shunted into a siding. Trains are also regarded as phallic symbols, or may relate to an individual's 'train of thought'.

If you dream you are travelling on public transport, just one of hundreds in a faceless mass of humanity, you have surrendered control of your journey and, to an extent, have allowed others to direct your progress. The reasons for this vary – it may simply be more convenient and provide a secure and reliable means of progress, or alternatively, the dreamer may feel

that their free expression and freedom of movement is hampered. Dreams about being on the wrong train reflect worries about one's role in life—the dreamer may be plagued by doubts about his life choices and want to get off the train. Overcrowded trains that are impossible to board reflect a

Large vehicles have always exerted a fascination, as people long to drive them, thrilled by the potential power they can control. Planes, buses and trains are the most popular forms of public transport in which individual travellers lose their identity, so a dream about travelling in this manner may reflect fears about losing one's individuality.

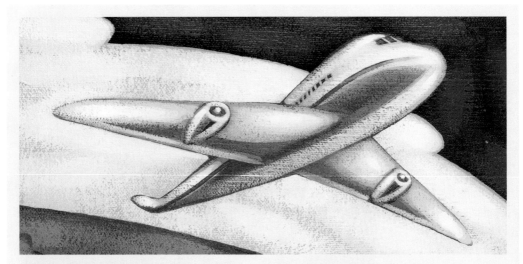

Flying in a passenger aircraft probably indicates a desire to travel, to leave behind the familiar and seek out exotic new places.

dreamer's lack of confidence or reluctance to compete with colleagues: once the train departs, the dreamer is left behind.

For most people, piloting a plane remains a fond ambition, but in dreams it represents our need to fly high above our peers, perhaps to excel and to chase our aspirations. It might be symptomatic of a need to leave behind the mundane ties of earth and to sample the freedom of the skies; this is especially likely if you find yourself flying with friends. Solo flight is more likely to be a sign of ambition.

Ships, boats, and yachts – journeys across seas or rivers – usually represent an emotional journey as water symbolises the unconscious mind. Boats can be mechanically powered, or dependent on the elements for motive power. They provide stability and protection while we are on the water and, like other vehicles, may represent the dreamer. Journeys across water provide us with a different view of the land and as symbols of the journey through life, provide a much wider perspective than a journey along a simple road. The condition of the water – be it calm, choppy, or stormy –

The sea is a primeval image which Freud and Jung used to symbolise the dreamer's emotional life.

Like cars, boats may symbolise the dreamer's personality, but as they travel over water, usually represent the dreamer's emotional journey.

signifies the dreamer's state of mind. A dream about skimming across the waves in a fast powerboat implies that the dreamer may be ignoring deep-seated emotions in his unconscious mind, whereas a dream about piloting a small yacht powered by the wind and waves suggests that the dreamer has closer contact with the elements and therefore his most powerful feelings. A dream in which you power a canoe suggests self-reliance and the ability to cope without the help of anyone else, and a dream about handling oars implies that you will set aside your own feelings to help others. If you dream

Rowboats are powered by the oarsmen, so this image represents a dreamer who confronts his emotional needs and deals with them purposefully.

160

that you are going off to sea, it may represent a journey into the unknown away from the familiarity of land and all that you hold dear; perhaps you want to leave home and all the restrictions imposed by family responsibilities. You may simply dream of standing on a beach while gazing out to sea as you ponder whether to 'take the plunge' and embark on an aquatic adventure (see page 201).

A tropical beach seems like paradise to many people, but the meeting of land and sea also represents the point where everyday life meets the dreamer's emotions.

Dreams of sea journeys by night rank among the most profound. Fraught with danger, travelling at sea by night requires mental strength and sound self-knowledge, just as in Greek mythology when individuals journeying to the underworld along the River Styx had to overcome their fear of death and abandon all egotistical ambitions. A stormy ocean implies that relationships will be equally turbulent, whereas a calm sea suggests serenity and peace. The prospect of a harbour signifies a safe resting place and may symbolise good news.

There are many metaphors about 'safe harbours', which are places of shelter for ships and boats, as well as being points of departure for sea travellers.

Portals

Docks, harbours, stations and airports are all points of arrival and departure, places of impermanence where people linger for a short time before embarking on a new adventure. They are the link between the old life and the challenges of the future. These transitional places often feature in anxiety dreams where the dreamer struggles and fails to catch a train, plane or bus, hampered by tedious barriers such as breakdowns, strikes or missed connections.

There is something faintly exciting, even exotic, about a busy station or airport which buzzes with purpose, and the feeling that people are resolutely moving through on to their next appointment. This sensation contrasts strongly with the atmosphere of a terminal crowded with stressed passengers who face hours of unexplained and interminable delays. Your dream termini reflect your attitude

An airport is a point of transition and can represent apprehension about the journey ahead, and thus the dreamer's future.

to change and progress in your life: do you stride purposefully through the station to catch the train that will take you to pastures new, or are you one of the apprehensive and dejected crowds glumly contemplating the 'flight delayed' section of the information screens?

Sigmund Freud believed that all dream journeys were reminders of death, and certainly if a departure is the focus of the dream, this may well be true. After the death of someone close, many people have experienced dreams featuring their loved one crossing a bridge, or standing on a threshold as they say goodbye.

Dreams about the start of journeys are more common than dreams about the journey's end, and running for a train is a classic anxiety dream. It reflects the dreamer's fears that he or she will miss the opportunities symbolised by the train journey.

Tunnels link two previously separate places, forging artificial, but sturdy, links between them.

Dreams are full of images of transition, such as doorways, staircases, gateways, bridges and tunnels, all of which represent connections as well as change. We are often faced with doors or gates that shut us off from whatever is behind them; if they are locked we may feel excluded or irritated. Sometimes we are slightly relieved that we cannot pass through as we do not want to face whatever is hidden. They can open on to absolutely anything, from pastoral visions to dank cellars, so

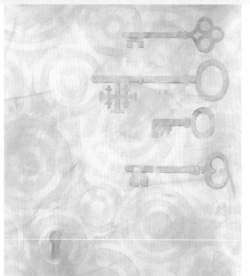

A locked door may induce feelings of exclusion, frustration or curiosity as to what is on the other side.

opening a dream door and stepping through it is a courageous act. If the door is locked, finding the key may be a problem, possibly one which we refuse to face as we do not want to confront whatever is behind the door. Gates often signify the dividing line between this world and the next; an open gate may represent opportunities, while a closed gate emphasises the lack of them. Try to overcome the obstacle by climbing over the gate and you may find that the impediment to your progress disappears.

Gates are barriers which must be surmounted or opened in order to move on. An open gate is inviting and hints at 'pastures new' or new opportunities.

Bridges may be symbols of change as they span the gap between the past and the future.

Bridges usually allow a clearer view of what is ahead and represent communication, linking the dreamer with others or with new experiences. They may symbolise transition as the dreamer leaves one phase of his life to cross to another. The structure of the bridge may be important here; a flimsy bridge does not inspire confidence and may represent the dreamer's fears about what he is about to do. A shiny strong structure with clear views of the land ahead is indicative of optimism for the future and of self-confidence, while a broken bridge indicates unfulfilled ambitions, plans that have failed and feelings of isolation. Dreams about passing under a bridge are more unusual and indicate uncertainty or instability in your life.

Tunnels are another means of communication, but they are subterranean and in dream analogy often symbolise the birth canal, the original tunnel through which we have all travelled to face the unknown. They also stand for access to the unconscious and often for optimism, as there is usually light at the end.

165

Chapter 5

Dream Places

*'What an air of probability sometimes
runs through a dream! And at others,
what a heap of absurdities it is!'*

Jane Austen *Emma*

The backdrop of a dream is almost as important in dream interpretation as the events themselves. Buildings of all kinds appear in our dreams, from the familiar domestic environment of our home or place of work, to institutions such as hospitals or schools, to mystical creations dreamed up by the subconscious. Many people dream of the place where they grew up, especially if they had a happy childhood.

Your dream buildings may or may not be familiar and, perhaps on waking, you will remember some of the more unlikely structures and be astonished at what your mind created. Fantastical or futuristic buildings are signs of a healthy imagination and an optimistic outlook on life as they show that the dreamer is forward-looking. Dreams of old buildings, such as churches or castles, denote a reverence for the past and a respect for tradition and ritual, although the context of the dream may signify that the dreamer is too rooted in his or her past and should look to his or her current situation for inspiration. Dreams about exploring buildings are often a sign that you should examine facets of your own personality in order to develop new skills and talents; a dream in which you discover unfamiliar rooms in a building you already know well is a classic dream and may occur at a time of change in your life.

The house

Jung was the first dream interpreter to identify a house as 'the mansion of the soul', in other words as a representation of the dreamer, with each room relating to a different aspect of the personality.

Many cultures have identified the house as representing the dreamer. Carl Jung was the first analyst to define the house as 'the mansion of the soul,' although the metaphor is common throughout Western literature. Just as human beings are multi-faceted creatures with different emotions and desires, so a house consists of inter-connecting rooms, each with its own particular function.

Jung's theories were based on a dream of his own. He dreamt of a large house and wandered around it, finding a cellar full of ancient remains, a comfortable sitting room and a rather dark, panelled ground floor. He related the dream house to the house in which he grew up with his religious parents. As he grew older and learnt more of comparative religions, Jung began to reject the religion of his youth, represented by the dark ground floor of his dream house. He believed that the cellar reflected his belief in the collective unconscious and the living room the fact that he had resolved the conflicts between the two belief systems.

Dreams that feature your own home and trivial events are extremely common. The appearance of your house usually symbolises protection, comfort and a need to be surrounded by familiar things. The condition of the house indicates your state of mind, as well as your hopes and fears for the future. So, a well-ordered house that appears comfortable reflects a balanced mind, not unduly worried about life. A disordered home with misplaced furniture, appliances that are the wrong size and rooms filled with strangers implies confusion and a need to examine a problem from a new perspective. The house that appears in the dream may not be the dreamer's real home, but its condition or style will still reflect the dreamer's self-image. A palace probably speaks for itself, while a dilapidated building shows a person who lacks self-esteem.

Although many dreams conjure up majestic buildings, perhaps with labyrinthine interiors and enormous rooms, most dreamscapes are drawn from more familiar buildings.

Each room within the house serves a different purpose and represents different aspects of the human personality. The kitchen is a vital nerve centre, symbolising nurture. The condition of a dream kitchen often provides a strong clue as to the dreamer's state of mind. A well-stocked, orderly kitchen reflects a competent individual with the resources to look after him or herself. Cooking is usually equated with hard work and good times enjoyed with loved ones. A dream which features continual cooking and domestic drudgery expresses feelings of distress – perhaps the dreamer feels undervalued by those around him or her? If the dream kitchen is stark and bare, a dreamer may be suffering from a lack of emotional or intellectual stimulation – it is time to go shopping for new interests. A kettle denotes domestic happiness, whereas a knife may be a warning: perhaps someone is about to stab you metaphorically in the back? The shape of ovens is reminiscent of the womb and may feature as the pun 'a bun in the oven' meaning that a woman is pregnant. Interestingly, dreams about baking have been related to conception.

Kitchens are places where we refuel physically and often mentally. It is a place of nourishment, so a dream about a kitchen full of delicious cooking aromas implies that the dreamer is emotionally happy and fulfilled. An empty cold kitchen suggests that the dreamer needs food for his soul.

Individual items within rooms enjoy their own symbolism. Kettles represent domestic contentment and a happy family life.

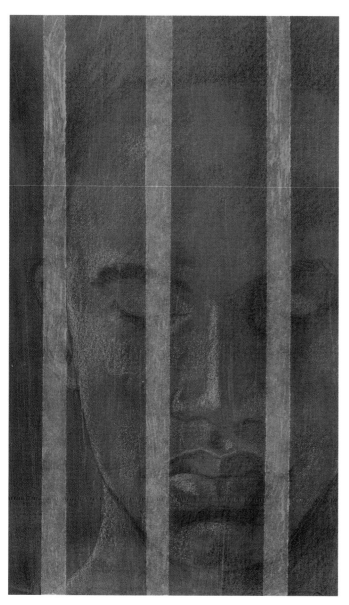

Basements or cellars are used for storage; they represent our memory, where we place things we may need one day, and other items that we wish to forget about. Occasionally, we find something in the cellar – welcome or unwelcome – which we had forgotten about. Dark, dank cellars can symbolise repression or the suppression of unwanted memories; light and airy basements are perhaps less cluttered, and reflect the dreamer's healthier mental state. If your dream cellar seems oppressive, confront whatever is causing the problem and try to tidy it up or clear it out.

Bars on a window represent imprisonment, and a feeling of constriction.

Living rooms – usually on the ground floor – relate to current circumstances and the conscious mind. They are public rooms used for entertaining, socialising and relaxing, so the ideal room is welcoming and bright. A dark, cramped living room suggests that the dreamer is unhappy with some aspect of his public self.

Furniture that is in good repair indicates happiness and contentment. Dreams about moving furniture reflect the desire or need to balance your commitments. Furniture that is in poor condition warns of love or marriage problems.

The living room is a public room where we entertain and represent the conscious mind and the present. The state of the living room therefore provides important clues about the dreamer's mental state.

Although it has a utilitarian purpose, furniture is also decorative and its state of repair reflects the dreamer's self-esteem: tatty tables and chairs imply that the dreamer should take more care with their appearance and learn to value themselves more highly.

Some analysts, like Jung, believe that a dream about gazing out of windows means that the dreamer is using his curiosity about the outside word as a substitute for self-analysis. Freud, however, regarded them as female sexual symbols.

The windows of a house are also important as they look out on to the world around, while giving outsiders the chance to look in. In dreams, they are the eyes of the building. Shuttered or curtained windows suggest a blinkered or introverted attitude to life, while large sun-filled windows reflect a desire to embrace the world outside. Dreams of opening windows express a desire to widen horizons, or perhaps to increase the flow of fresh air or new opinions through your house or soul. If you dream of peering into the windows of a building, you may be trying to examine a particular aspect of your personality; or if it is clearly the house of someone else, perhaps you are trying to get closer to a friend.

Staircases provide access to the upper floors of a house, which represent the spiritual side of the mind. A dream about climbing a staircase may signify a spiritual or emotional mission, while dreams of descending stairs show that the dreamer wishes to explore an aspect of his past or subconscious. A wide-open staircase symbolises an easy path to achievement, whereas a dark, winding set of stairs is a sign that the journey may be more difficult.

In dreams, stairs enable dreamers to progress up towards their ambitions, or to descend into the basement of their soul to examine their subconscious.

The bedroom is possibly the most important room in the house for a dedicated student of dream interpretation.

Water in dreams often symbolises emotional life, so bathrooms, with all their scatological connotations, often reflect the dreamer's feelings and sensitivities.

Attics at the top of a house are where we store junk, old possessions or much-loved mementoes; in one sense they are similar to cellars as they represent the recesses of the mind, but they also look out on to the sky and the heavens and therefore reflect our highest aspirations.

Bedrooms relate to close relationships and beds themselves can be places of refuge or an indication of the state of a marriage. If you dream you are in bed with a strange person, it could be that they represent a partner in business or an aspect of a troubling problem. Animals in bed are signs of bad luck, while dreams of bed bugs imply illness and possibly loss. Bathrooms, which are private places of cleansing, are where we confront ourselves honestly and examine problems and faults. Water is an important element in a bathroom, (see page 123) as it embodies the Christian symbolism of washing away sins and purging ourselves of guilt. Dreams of being seen using a lavatory in public reflect fears of exposure or vulnerability; the dreamer must try to take control of the situation that worries them. Floods in bathrooms represent a sense of being overwhelmed: order must be restored by looking at the situation more objectively. Dreams of warm baths show emotional stability, security and prosperity, but cold baths sometimes indicate loss and instability. Soap, slippery, perfumed or foul tasting, symbolises a puzzle or enigma. A shower may denote creativity, as water is the life force that stimulates us.

The garden around a house is also important, as it represents the inner life that the dreamer is cultivating. The colours of the garden reflect the dreamer's mental state (see pages 68–70), while an arid, weed-strewn garden shows that the dreamer has an empty emotional life. If the garden is formally laid out, examine the shapes of the bed and lawns, as their pattern may be important. A walled garden is a sign that the dreamer has an area of his life that he wishes to keep completely private, perhaps even from his closest friends and family. A vegetable garden, which is often hard to cultivate, is a sign that you must persevere in order to realise your ambitions. A garden filled with flowers is a sign of optimism and good news. A kennel in the garden indicates that someone is not responding to your charm – a kennel is

Soap puns may crop up in dreams: the dreamer might be confused, cross, or 'in a lather', or may have memories of being told to 'wash their mouth out in soap and water' as a punishment for being rude. Slippery, foul-tasting, yet fragrantly perfumed, soap is a baffling substance and sometimes symbolises puzzles.

Gardens can also be personal spaces where people spend time nurturing and caring for plants. In dreams gardens may represent the dreamer's interior life, his deepest thoughts and secret hopes; a well cultivated garden implies a rich inner life.

part of your dream landscape, but not in an intimate way.

A HOUSE DREAM

This dream, in which the dreamer's house is critical, provides an interesting comment upon the dreamer's fears about her reputation.

'I was collecting blackberries on my allotment when a matt black diamond-shaped spaceship hovered above it and vacuumed up all the weeds. Initially pleased, I was less happy when I was sucked into the spaceship, too. I was worried because it was only the thickness of a credit card and I wondered how I would fit in. I don't remember what the interior looked like, but I was released unharmed. When I got home I was upset to find the spaceship spitting the allotment weeds out all over my house.'

Interpretation: The background to this is that dreamer had discovered that she had been implicated in a local scandal through no fault of her own. Although entirely innocent, she feared that people were discussing her behind her back. The black spaceship is a diamond shape, which in Jungian analysis represents the Self. To the dreamer it appears thin and possibly fragile, but it is clearly immensely strong: this should reassure the dreamer that she is above suspicion and has strong inner resources to cope with the situation, despite her figurative fear of being rejected by her neighbours. The house represents the dreamer herself, so throwing weeds on the house shows a fear of being showered with insults by the neighbours. She should remember that weeds are pretty harmless, and will soon decompose; similarly the offensive comments will disappear very quickly.

Dreams about moving house, or looking for a new home, imply an unsettled state of mind. The dreamer may want to make a fresh start and put certain aspects of his life or personality well and truly behind him. A dream about looking around the houses of other people suggests an open, perhaps even inquisitive nature and the desire to become more closely involved with those around you.

It is a well-known fact that moving house is one of life's more stressful experiences, so a dream about moving may simply reflect this anxiety. However, if the dream house represents the dreamer, moving house may signify the dreamer's desire to reinvent himself in some way.

Caves were the first human homes, so in a dream they may hark back to primitive living and the dreamer's desire to simplify his life and surroundings. Their shape resembles the womb, so the dreamer may want to recapture the protection and comfort of the months before birth. They can also be damp places, and some dream interpreters believe that they are a warning to take care of your health.

A dream about living in a cave may symbolise the dreamer's desire for a more simple life. Caves are ancient human homes and cave-dwellers experience life at its most elemental.

Doors, locks and keys

Keys have great symbolic meaning as they provide the means to unlock things, both actually and metaphorically. Some people dream about keys when they are struggling over an intellectual problem in their waking life.

Doors and gates always represent transitions; they provide access to other places, a different spiritual level, and new opportunities. The dreamer must pass through a doorway to move on and progress to his or her future, and this very act requires assurances and confidence. Sometimes doors are locked, with whatever lies behind them remaining a mystery. If the dreamer has lost the key, he may not wish to confront whatever is behind the door – this reflects a fear of what the future holds.

Apart from their primary use, keyholes provide an opportunity to spy on others, and so provide a dream warning to keep an eye on the activities of your colleagues or friends. Keys are important dream symbols. A key inserted into a lock can symbolise love – the fusion of two perfectly matched individuals, the unlocking of your soul or, more crudely, sexual love. A broken key suggests that success has eluded you, and If you dream of giving a key away, you may lose your good reputation. There are many metaphors about keys, such as finding the key to a problem or the keys to someone's heart, and keys are often related to gaining access to something or unlocking a problem.

Public buildings

Schools, offices, shops, hospitals, churches and other buildings, can all play a significant part in dreams. Once again, the dreaming mind may have summoned them simply for a straightforward purpose, but they may also have more subtle meanings.

Churches are obviously associated with religion, their spires pointing to the sky and the higher reaches of consciousness. They are often ancient, dark buildings with spaces suddenly pierced by light shining through beautiful stained glass. A church in a dream indicates a place of reflection and assessment, perhaps the need to reconnect with your spiritual side. Temples or other religious sanctuaries have similar meanings and, like churches, imply ritual, which many people find comforting, although others may find it oppressive. If a religious

Churches are buildings of peace, ritual and tranquility, and it is these aspects that reassure many people. Others, however, may dislike the formality. Dream churches may seem oppressive, or may be a hint that the dreamer should contemplate the spiritual side of his nature.

building looms large in a dream, consider the various shapes of the spires, domes and other architectural features, as they may also have significance (see pages 78–83).

Arches, for example, are symbols of unity as they support two pillars. Arches may also be monuments in their own right – testaments to victory or military success – so they may represent the dreamer's status and public recognition of his achievements. Passing through a dream arch can be empowering. Fallen arches are negative symbols, however, and imply that the dreamer's hopes will not be realised.

To Western dreamers, temples may appear exotic, or simply be reminders of holidays. However, Hindu dreamers are more likely to associate them with their religious life.

Arches are unifying shapes which link two pillars. If the dreamer finds himself underneath an arch, he may crave the same sort of protection the arch provides.

Columns are vital parts of ecclesiastical architecture as they support the roof, so a dream column may emphasise the responsibilities of the dreamer in supporting himself or his family. They soar heavenwards and may also symbolise the dreamer's spiritual aspirations. More obviously, columns are phallic symbols, although if they are broken or crumbling disaster is on the horizon.

Dreams of aisles may be about weddings, but may also denote a feeling of being trapped in a situation over which you have little control. Altars are symbols of great ritual, but may signal the need for an apology, reflecting perhaps the need for forgiveness of sins. Although graveyards and cemeteries have faintly morbid connotations, dreams of burial places are not uncommon and are often considered to be a sign of optimism after recovering from an illness or emerging from a tricky situation at home or work. They are rarely a sign of impending death either for the dreamer or loved ones, and may just point to a need to think about the past or family members.

Pillars play a critical supporting role in many large buildings, so pillars and columns may form a pun in dreams relating to 'tower of strength', 'pillar of the community'.

The aisles of a church most obviously conjure up images of a bride and groom 'going down the aisle'. Long, clear passages, they ensure that anyone using them makes a very public entrance, and this kind of exposure may seem like a nightmare for shy, sensitive souls.

183

Castles are often impregnable fortresses, and are sometimes the stuff of fairy tales. Dreamers may long for the security of a castle, or may dream about attacking it, perhaps using it to symbolise a long-standing problem.

Castles may reflect aspirations or wish fulfilment: the dreamer may want to live somewhere larger or more secure. Freud believed that castles represented unattainable women, so if a man dreams of besieging a castle, it might imply sexual frustration.

Law courts are often imposing buildings, symbols of state power, and of law and order. The court itself is a place of ritual, where one person, the judge, can determine the freedom or imprisonment of a person. Law courts can be an expression of the dreamer's powers of discretion and judgement, or possibly a fear that their crimes will catch up with them. If a lawyer appears in your dreams, it may be a hint to seek specialist advice, legal or otherwise. Dreams of justice, especially of juries, denote criticism – perhaps the dreamer fears the opinions of his peers – although some analysts believe that a dream featuring the scales of justice are a sign of a successful future.

Most people dream about their childhood and schools may feature in dreams like this. They may also remind the dreamer of happy memories or help to underline how life has moved on and improved.

Schools and libraries relate to learning, although if an adult dreams of school, he or she is probably harking back to his or her youth and the pain or pleasure inherent in that period. Schools often feature in dreams about lost youth and forgotten opportunities, or they may imply that the dreamer should pay attention to the intellectual side of his nature. Blackboards in dreams may be a sign that interesting news is on the horizon; look carefully at any writing on the blackboard and try to make sense of it. Many people have recurring dreams about sitting important exams, years after they have successfully passed them and this is simply an anxiety dream, probably occurring at times of self-doubt.

Offices and factories are impersonal buildings, and in dreams may depict certain aspects of the dreamer's character. Dreams of working on a factory production line or as one of thousands of staff in an impersonal office, for example, may reflect fears about a loss of individuality or identity. On the other hand, factories are also places where things are made, so may represent creativity and new ideas. Offices denote hierarchy, power and

Exams often feature as part of an anxiety dream, perhaps many years after the examination has been successfully completed.

Factories are increasingly automated and a dream about working on a production line raises questions about the dreamer's feeling of individuality.

Full-time workers may spend more time in the office with their co-workers than with their families. Dreamers who resent this may dream about the office as a place of oppression, even a prison.

money; they are places where information is filed and money is made, although they can also be places of repression and boredom.

Shops appear in many guises in dreams. If you dream you are running a profitable and popular shop, it denotes your own success, but if it lacks customers or is poorly organizsed, you should examine your lifestyle and the way others perceive you. Dreams of going shopping reflect your attitude to possessions. An airy shopping centre full of attractive shops shows an optimistic dreamer able to take advantage of whatever life has to offer. A dream of standing in front of a shop window filled with desirable but unattainable items reflects a feeling of exclusion from the luxuries of life and perhaps a problem of low self-worth.

Shops peddle dreams and often appeal to peoples' aspirations. Dreamers need to ask themselves what they are shopping for, as the goods may represent something that the dreamer feels is missing from his or her life.

A shopping centre is a busy, often impersonal place. A dream mall would presumably be full of shops giving their wares away!

Hospitals may be an indication of the dreamer's fears of ill health in himself or loved ones. They can also be about the surrender of control: in hospital we give ourselves up to the care of medical professionals who literally have the power of life or death over patients. Some dreamers may relish the fact that someone else can take responsibility for their life and enjoy the feeling of security this gives them, while others will abhor the idea of this loss of self-determination. If you dream that you are a heroic doctor with life-saving skills, this is probably a cry for recognition in your work, or a desire to take on more responsibility in one area of your life, and is a common wish-

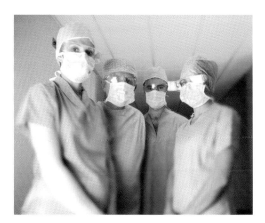

Hospitals can be intimidating places, especially if the dreamer believes that he or someone close to him is gravely ill. A dream about being a doctor implies that the dreamer wants to be a hero, to earn the praise accorded to skilled surgeons and medical staff.

Places of unlimited knowledge, libraries embody past episodes in the dreamer's life.

fulfilment dream. Asylums are misunderstood places, and in dreams they mean that you or a close companion will run into difficulties; you may be required to help a friend through their problems.

Libraries and museums, stuffed with books, exhibits and curios, are about the past and memories. What exactly do you see in your dream museum? These are sources of unlimited knowledge and books may represent episodes of the dreamer's life.

Theatres and concert halls are places where human life is dramatised in words and song, and where human passions and foibles are exaggerated, examined and finally exhausted in the space of a few hours. Dreams themselves are mini-dramas, which entertain us for short periods of time and help us to interpret our lives and feelings. Cinemas are places of escapism and fantasy where we can all dream of lives in parallel universes. The dreamer may become involved in the film or could just be a voyeur to the action.

Unless you are a keen actor, dreams of performing in front of an audience are usually about how you appear to those around you. Is your dream performance confident and does the audience applaud or boo? The audience usually represents friends and family and the identity of individual members may hold important clues when trying to unravel the meaning of the dream. In addition, note what sort of dream play you were performing in – comedy or tragedy? If you dream of preparing yourself for a performance by putting on costumes and make-up, you are probably hiding some part of yourself from others during your waking life. Dreams about theatres may be a sign that you should exercise caution and refrain from speaking too openly about your plans.

A dream about performing in front of an appreciative audience may mean that the dreamer wants recognition and appreciation for his achievements. Alternatively, the prospect of standing up in front of hundreds of people may be terrifying and take on all the characteristics of a nightmare.

Chapter 6

The World Around Us

'It must be very peaceful, he thought, to lie and slumber and dream forever and ever, with the wind whispering through the trees and caressing the grass and the flowers over the grave, and nothing to bother and grieve about, ever any more.'

Mark Twain *Adventures of Tom Sawyer*

Landscape

You may be aware that the landscape of your dream is more important than any buildings, and perhaps the most critical thing here is the dreamer's reaction to that landscape. We are all accustomed to different environments, so will react differently to the scenery around us, and imaginative, creative people may well conjure up more scenic and fantastic landscapes than more practical souls. Many artists have been inspired by the landscapes of their dreams and the works of surrealists, such as Salvador Dali, are particularly dream-like. Indeed, Dali worked hard to encourage his unconscious to produce fantastic landscapes by dozing in a chair, his chin in his hand and his elbow on a table. In this way, when his chin dropped he awoke from a hypnogogic sleep which had been full of bizarre images and surreal images which he then employed in his paintings.

Cities symbolise the community and the dreamer's relationship with it, so if you dream of wandering around an anonymous urban landscape, you may well feel alienated from those around you in your daily life. Similarly, a dream where you can see a city but are unable to reach or enter it reflects feelings of exclusion. If, however, your dream city is one of soaring towers and shimmering glass palaces, you may have high ideals and expect the same from your colleagues. Misty, indistinct buildings may indicate a dreamer's lack of understanding of others, or express his or her unease in personal relationships. Futuristic cities are generally a sign of optimism and happiness: the dreamer looks towards a bright future with great hope and expectations. Visiting a strange city in your dreams may infer that circumstances will force a house move.

The mood of a dream is often dependent on the background or landscape. One cityscape may appear threatening and soulless, while another may be vibrant and packed with opportunities and challenges.

The rolling countryside, ordered fields, small villages and green hills may be comforting to some, and claustrophobic to others. Agriculture is the lifeblood of the country, producing the foodstuffs so necessary to everyone, so dreams set in an agricultural setting may relate to the dreamer's whole life and what he needs for both physical and spiritual sustenance.

The environment of a dream has a strong bearing on its atmosphere, and the weather, landscape and general surroundings are often critical factors in trying to unravel its meaning. The time of year and the background scenery may reinforce the action of the dream, or may alternatively imply something completely different which becomes clear only after careful reflection. The weather or season may enhance the mood, or completely alter what appears to be a familiar landscape. In medieval times, soothsayers and astrologers used the four elements – fire, earth, water and air – to assign characteristics to people's personalities and each element can assume different forms in dreams.

A dream featuring farming or agriculture may relate to the dreamer's basic need for nurture.

Weather and the elements

Fire, one of the four 'elements' described by medieval philosophers, is changeable, hot, beautiful and dangerous. A dream fire may remind the dreamer of passionate feelings, or alternatively, warn him or her from a project that is 'too hot to handle'.

Fire traditionally represents passion, creativity and sometimes danger. There is a world of difference between the warm fire burning in the grate and a forest fire growing wildly out of control; in dream symbolism the first represents a love of one's domestic situation, the second a person in crisis, overwhelmed by passion and feelings. Brightly burning flames in a fireplace are an expression of a healthy imagination. If you dream of getting burnt by fire, you must guard against losing your temper. A dream in which you set fire to a

house may be a sign of self-loathing and deep anger – the house represents the dreamer's soul – so try to work out what is making you so angry. Fire is a transforming force, altering everything it touches, so it is also a symbol of change and sometimes destruction. Smoke is often considered an unlucky sign and some dream interpreters believe that slowly twisting smoke is a sign of death.

A dream about a burning house suggests that the dreamer fears being consumed by his feelings.

Gusts of air during dreams might enable the dreamer to fly, to soar above everyday life towards the heavens.

Air symbolised otherworldliness in medieval times and, in dreams, relates to spirituality, freedom, wisdom and the higher self. A gentle breeze felt during a dream may represent the life force, whereas a strong wind is far more perturbing and may signify change. Breezes often enable the dreamer to float gently among dream clouds, surveying everything below them and gaining a new perspective on life around them. The comfort and satisfaction of this may be ended abruptly by sudden gusts of strong wind, buffeting the dreamer back down to earth with a bump. A dream about being blown about by the wind represents surrender to forces too powerful for the individual to control. Storms often whip up rubble or blow away possessions, so dream storms may be a sign of inner conflict between the rational self and spiritual feelings; strong winds may blow away old beliefs, making room for changed attitudes. Hurricanes are frightening, yet magnificent, natural phenomena which rip through landscapes and cities with no mercy; not surprisingly, in dreams they represent confrontation and quarrelling. Storms stir up confusion, while a lightning strike may

Air and breezes suggest clarity, freedom and spirituality; such dreams may be 'a breath of fresh air'.

The onset of storms is heralded by a heavy, thunderous atmosphere as the sky darkens. The calm before the storm is often followed by mayhem as heavy winds and torrential rain wreck the landscape. Storms symbolise the unexpected forces that can turn dreamers' lives upside down.

Beautiful and colourful, rainbows are universal symbols of optimism, forgiveness and good luck.

illuminate the situation and provide clarity. As a powerful natural force beyond the control of humans, lightning is often associated with intuition and messages from the gods and is the symbol of revelation.

Rainbows appear when the atmospheric mix of air and water allows light to refract into a glorious spectrum of colour. They are always symbols of optimism and even if we know that there are not really any pots of gold, there is at least a chance that the sun will come out and the rain will stop for the day!

A rainy day is often depressing and rain may represent tears in dreams, especially if the dreamer feels rain dripping gently down his or her face.

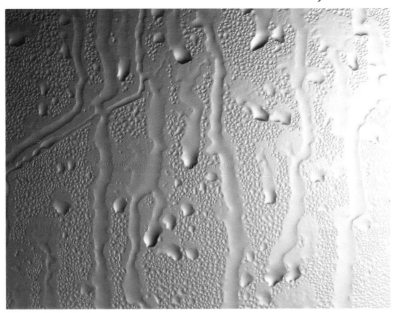

Although umbrellas offer protection against the elements, in dreams they may warn of misunderstandings to come.

Rain is usually a factor in storms and water is regarded as a purifying life force relating, in dreams, to the emotions and unconscious mind. Rain is often an indication of tears or unhappiness. Undeniably we need rain to survive, but there is something miserable about a wet, grey day, and in dream interpretation rain implies depression and suggests that the dreamer should pay more attention to his or her emotional life. It may hint at intellectual or emotional renewal. A sudden shower on a hot day implies that you have minor emotional troubles, but a downpour implies more serious problems that need attention. A variation on this theme is a dream about a house, which leaks when it rains: again the message is that you must examine your unconscious mind for emotional issues that are struggling for attention.

A dream lake and its setting may represent the dreamer's attitude to his deep emotional life: a well-used lake surrounded by a beautiful park suggests a dreamer who pays attention to the needs of his subconscious mind, whereas a lake in an arid landscape implies neglect.

Water appears in dream landscapes as the sea, lakes, streams, rivers or as ice. Rivers may symbolise the dreamer's passage through life (see page 54), whereas streams or springs often represent ideas, especially if they contain fish or other creatures. Pools, ponds or lakes can be places of contemplation, peace and revitalisation. We all enjoy a dip in a cool pool on a hot day or stumbling upon a small lake while on a walk. In dream terminology the dreamer is being encouraged to spend time just thinking about himself. If you see your reflection in a pool of water, this may be a confrontation with your 'shadow' (see page 63). The image beamed back at you may be unflattering or even unrecognisable, and may embody an aspect of your character that you rarely face; sometimes, aquatic creatures such as mermaids may try to lure you under water.

A dream about swimming in a pool may relate to the dreamer's attitude to life and how he copes with challenges. The dreamer may approach life by 'going with the flow', which ensures that everything goes 'swimmingly'.

If your dream pond is murky or muddy, however, it may symbolise the presence of a problem that is causing mixed feelings in one area of your life. Marshy areas combine earth and water. In dream analysis mud becomes a substance that causes confusion and conflict between our rational selves and our emotional inclinations. Perhaps you feel that something is 'dragging you down'? Quicksand symbolises sticky situations from which it may be difficult to extract yourself. In a similar way, a dream set on the seashore or a beach imply a link between the conscious mind and the subconscious. These are places of renewal and revitalisation, as the shore is washed clean every day by the tide. Beaches and tropical islands are often literally 'dream destinations' where people long to escape. Jung believed that a dream about looking out to sea meant that the dreamer was prepared to confront the forces of the subconscious. Dreams about the seaside may also hark back to the simple pleasures of childhood holidays. A lighthouse is a beacon of safety that looks out over water; in a dream this may signify a point of security that the dreamer is striving towards while struggling with emotional turmoil. It is

Sandy beaches are reminiscent of family holidays, so in dreams may simply conjure up nostalgic childhood memories.

Lighthouses are beacons of safety, shining their lights out over the sea, or in dream terminology, the emotional life. They provide direction for the dreamer.

Stormy seas reflect turbulent emotions in dreams.

If water represents feelings, ice symbolises
frozen emotions, perhaps a person bereft of
love.

also a tower and in Freudian
terminology, this would represent a
phallic symbol. Perhaps you should also
consider whether you are trying to warn
someone away from you.

Water can be a powerful natural force,
overwhelming storm defences; you may
dream about being tossed on a stormy
sea and both of these images suggest
that emotions are rising to the surface,
which had previously been kept under
control, hidden by the conscious mind.
Although storms, floods and other
watery images may stir up unwanted
feelings, they are healthier dreams than
those featuring cold, icy landscapes. Ice
symbolises frozen emotions, or a part of
your life that has been 'put on ice' or
neglected for a time. A dream about
climbing a glacier, travelling across an
icy, snowy landscape or ice-skating
implies that the dreamer is ignoring an
important part of his or her psyche by
skating over emotions.

There is nothing more beautiful than a
mountainous snowy landscape against
a brilliant blue sky, but this may be the
manifestation of a transforming dream,
and the symbolism of this is complex.

The snow-covered mountains imply that the dreamer must scale emotional heights to reach spiritual peace; snow symbolises emotional purity and the mountain peak is a challenge that must be overcome.

The earth traditionally represents reliability and solidity, strength and permanence. It may feature in dreams as the planet Earth, as seen from space – an image of startling beauty and strange familiarity – or in a more mundane manner as clumps of mud, perhaps even dreams about digging

The sharp, clean outline of a snow-capped mountain peak may symbolise spiritual purity: mountains represent our highest aims and the white snow, virtue.

A dream about digging suggests that the dreamer is searching for something; perhaps he or she is 'digging for roots', something to do with the past or family history.

the earth. This last group relates to creativity – ideas are planted and take root. If you dream about sitting or lying on the ground, this may reflect an urge to remain rooted in reality rather than flitting off on a flight of fancy.

The Earth is all around us, and its different landscapes radically alter the mood or meaning of dreams. Wide, open spaces are invigorating and endow a sense of freedom, enabling people to see for miles, really appreciating the elements. Fields and pastures may be a pun on 'field of

Fertile green pasture is a sign of optimism, new life and new ideas.

Dream deserts often suggest that the dreamer feels isolated, unloved and has an arid emotional life.

interest', perhaps one's job or hobbies. The condition of a field will reflect the strength of the dreamer's commitment to those interests, so a field full of crops signifies a strong interest, while one that is fallow indicates a distinct lack. A bleak landscape is not so stimulating and may reflect the dreamer's reluctance to engage with life around him. The most extreme form of this is a desert, which, as a dreamscape, implies emotional barrenness and an inability to find solace in human interaction. If you dream of an earthquake, beware, as your life is likely to be shaken up dramatically.

Deserts are endless, arid landscapes and may embody a sense of loss or that something is missing in the dreamer's life. They are often associated with long, hazardous journeys of a solitary nature. Many people, however, surrounded by the complexities of juggling stressful jobs and punishing schedules, may regard the peace and tranquility of an empty desert as highly desirable.

Forests, woods and jungles are teeming with plant and animal life and may appear forbidding or represent the unknown. Trees are often regarded as symbols of wisdom, so dreamers may walk in a forest for inspiration and guidance. If it is a particularly dense forest, make sure you can 'see the wood for the trees', in other words you need to sort through the extraneous parts of your life that impede clear decision-making. A dream about a small wood rather than a dense forest, relates to your family or the community around you. If the trees are well spaced, relationships are well balanced, but if the trees are widely separated, perhaps the dreamer is feeling distant from those around him. Damp and often threatening, jungles house dangerous

Forests may appear threatening, as trees hang low and hide all manner of frightening beasts. In many fairy tales, they represent the unknown and appear as an ever-present danger that is to be avoided at all costs.

Solitary trees embody endurance and strength; in some dreams they might stand for individual people.

205

animals, which may lurk in the undergrowth ready to hurt the dreamer. A dream of a jungle may be a warning not to become too involved in something complex and ultimately harmful.

Hills, mountains and cliffs often represent obstacles or problems that we must overcome in order to progress, or else they are pinnacles which we must reach in order to be fulfilled. If a dreamer experiences craggy landscapes night after night, they perhaps feel isolated and unable to communicate effectively with those around them. A dream about climbing a mountain shows that you are tackling your

problems in the most direct way possible, or that you are determined to achieve your ambitions. If you are faced with an abyss in your dream, beware. Teetering on the edge of a steep drop, scared of falling over the edge into endless blackness is a primordial fear, and at its most basic level, this type of dream is a warning to take care. The dreamer must consider how to surmount this obstacle without endangering his or herself; the abyss probably represents problems or quarrels that cannot be avoided. A view of a canyon, however, is breathtaking and represents the dreamer's ability to look rationally at his life from a lofty perspective.

There are two ways of viewing mountains: as obstacles in one's path, or as challenges to be overcome, and the action of the dream will probably underline the dreamer's approach. A canyon is at once breathtaking and dangerous and may represent unavoidable problems.

Seasonal rhythms

The dawn of a new day suggests new possibilities and opportunities as light turns the murky night into day.

The atmosphere of a dream is radically affected by the season, whether it is dark or light, dusk or dawn. The unchanging rhythms of nature influence us all and are factors with additional symbolic significance, which may help you to gain a deeper understanding of your dream.

Dawn is a time of optimism as we look forward to a new day; it is the hope we cling to during the darkness of night, certain that troubles will be cleared away by the first rays of sunshine. A sunrise may be a pun on the name Dawn, or provide the answer to a problem, as it 'dawns on' you. The sun is a powerful symbol in cultures throughout the world, a source of

The sun, which provides light, warmth and energy is an important symbol in many cultures and may represent wisdom, truth or God.

warmth, light and energy, and can represent the intellect and intelligence of the dreamer. It is regarded as a masculine symbol and a blazing sun indicates that your efforts will be successful. Artemidorus believed that dreams about the sun were good omens, 'except for those who want to keep something secret or hid'. Sunlight provides illumination and we all have sides of ourselves that we wish to keep hidden, so may not always relish our time in the sun. Dusk and sunset often symbolise the end of a life or the approach of old age and death.

The dark of night adds a sense of mystery to a dream, but it can also be confusing or even frightening in the dark. Darkness may signify the dark recesses of the unconscious mind.

Dreams set at a night suggest that the dreamer is suffering doubt, and is perhaps worried about being 'kept in the dark' about something. Darkness can seem menacing and the dreamer may be worried by what it hides. If the dreamscape is lit by the moon, the atmosphere will be calm and peaceful. Symbolic of spiritual wisdom, the moon relates to the feminine, intuitive side of our nature and helps to illuminate the unconscious mind; it is unattainable yet known to us all. A full moon radiates serenity, while a new moon signifies new projects. A starry night provides a

A full moon softly illuminates the night sky and has come to symbolise intuition, love and madness (lunacy).

beautiful and possibly romantic backdrop to a dream as stars represent hope and destiny. If one especially bright star is visible, the dream message may be to 'follow your star'. Shooting stars, which burn brightly across the night sky, are symbols of optimism and success, although meteors, which are a potential sources of damage, may hint at loss to come. Comets were traditionally regarded as bad omens and in dreams denote future problems.

Shooting stars burn brightly, but fizzle out quite quickly, rather like someone whose early promise remains unfulfilled.

Springtime is a season of hope and expectation, signifying the revival of life after winter. A dream set in the spring is usually one of happiness.

Autumn is a beautiful season as the leaves change colour and the harvest is gathered in. However, winter is on the horizon and autumn sometimes represents melancholy feelings.

The passage of the year is marked by the changing seasons, each of which has a symbolic meaning in dream interpretation. Spring is a time of renewal and growth. The sun becomes slowly warmer, driving away the winter frosts, and plants take root in the soil. Spring symbolises expectation, hope, and the development of new projects or ideas. It can also represent youth, childhood or our 'salad days'.

Summer is a time of consolidation and enjoyment of life. It may symbolise early adulthood and the 'prime of life'. As summer gives way to fall, the light fades and the temperature drops. At the same time, however, we harvest what we sowed in the spring and it is a time of plenty. Fall may represent the middle years of life, when humans are no longer in the first flush of youth but are still able to reap enjoyment from life. The harsh cold of winter, together with bleak landscapes of bare trees and frozen earth can be depressing. Remember, however, that crops and plants are still growing beneath the ground, so life is not entirely dead. Winter often symbolises old age and declining powers.

Trees and plant life

Trees are the oldest living things on our planet; some species of pine are thought to live for 5,000 years and so trees have become symbols of timelessness and wisdom. They may represent the family ('family tree'), with the roots symbolising ancestors and the branches the current members. The tree of knowledge is an important image in the book of Genesis in the Bible as it produces the forbidden fruit, which becomes man's downfall.

Trees can be phallic symbols, or may signify renewal, and evergreens in particular may represent eternal life. A healthy tree is an indication of prosperity, but brown, withered leaves suggest that you should find another means of earning money. A dream about climbing a tree implies that you are trying to rise above everyday life to

Trees may be regarded as phallic symbols, or as images of life and renewal.

find solace; alternatively, the dreamer should perhaps consider getting his feet back 'down to earth'. Felling a tree may symbolise ending a project or failing in your ambitions; it may signify the deliberate end of something.

Individual species have their own symbolism. Oak trees, for example, are venerable trees and in Celtic belief were regarded as holy. Both Celtic and Norse traditions endowed them with masculine qualities of strength and sexual power, the latter based partly on the mistletoe – an important fertility symbol – found on oaks in winter. Dreams about collecting acorns are a

Venerable, sturdy oaks are a symbol of England, and in broader terms, protection.

A glorious spring scene of blossom and burgeoning flowers is always a positive sign of optimism.

sign that you will acquire an unexpected amount of money and that prosperity is on the horizon.

Oaks remain symbols of stability and protection, especially within the family, while yew trees symbolise intractable family problems. They are also associated with death, partly because thy are often planted in cemeteries. Evergreen pines played an important part in pagan winter festivals and remain with us today as a symbol of Christmas. In dreams they may be nostalgic reminders of family Christmas celebrations or symbols of regeneration and fertility. Olive trees are the source of olive branches, which are a symbol of peace, so a dream featuring an olive tree is usually a sign of good fortune. Verdant and shady, fig trees have wonderful tactile leaves and have biblical associations, having been used to cover the nudity of Adam and Eve. The fig itself is regarded almost as an erotic fruit and a dream about figs and fig trees is likely to be a sensual experience.

Illuminated, gaudy Christmas trees brighten up winter when the days are at their shortest.

Blossom on trees is a sign of spring, renewal, and prosperity; they may be a sign of happiness and youthful pursuits, but like the blossom, these feelings of contentment will not last long. There may be a pun involved: perhaps a relationship or project is 'blossoming'? Flowers, fruit and vegetables also incorporate their own meanings in dreams. They may be general symbols of fruitfulness and fertility, or relate to sexuality because of their resemblance to genitalia. The condition of the flowers is critical: in bud, they are symbols of hope, in full flower they represent beauty and fulfilment, while withered or dying blooms are symbols of loathing or contempt. The ancient 'language of flowers' ascribes different meanings to various species. Flowers in a dream may also be read as a pun on a woman's name, such as Lily or Myrtle.

Lilies represent innocence, mercy and charity and dreams of this flower are a sign of spiritual health. Since the First World War, poppies have become a symbol of remembrance and death, as they flowered prolifically in the killing fields of northern France. However, because of the opium produced from the seeds, poppies have been associated with sleeping and death since ancient Greek times.

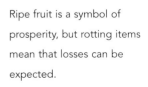

Ripe fruit is a symbol of prosperity, but rotting items mean that losses can be expected.

Roses symbolise love and a dozen red roses is the traditional gift of a young lover. They represent feminine beauty and virginity when in bud, but if thorns feature in your dream, there may be hostility in your relationship. The colour of a rose is important: white indicates purity, pink romance, red stands for fiery passion and a black rose means death.

Chrysanthemums are a sign of love and affection, but white flowers hint that a lover may leave you. Cheery yellow daffodils indicate that spring has arrived, and are a sign of good fortune. With their radiating petals imitating the rays of the sun, daisies may represent the sun and intelligence. They are scattered everywhere and often collected by children, so are also a sign of innocence. Dreams of heady purple lilac are associated with bad luck, even death; there is a

Stately, scented lilies stand for innocence and charity.

Roses are traditional symbols of love, but Freud believed that their tightly furled shape also represented female genitalia.

215

superstition that lilac should never be taken into a hospital or even the house. Graceful tulips may signify a secret or hasty marriage, or, as they are farmed on the Netherlands, may symbolise Holland. Violets denote love and affection, as well as modesty, as in 'shrinking violet'.

Succulent, naturally occurring sources of energy, fruit and vegetables are another symbol of fertility and plenty. They may indicate that a project or relationship is going well and 'bearing fruit'. A large collection of fruit and vegetables conjures up images of market stalls or harvest time, as long as the produce is ripe and fresh. An image of dried or rotten fruit is a bad omen.

Apples embody the ancient symbolism of the Bible, when Eve was tempted with an apple from the tree of knowledge.

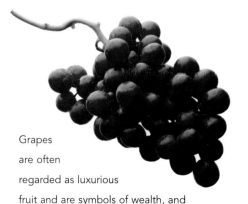

Grapes are often regarded as luxurious fruit and are symbols of wealth, and sometimes decadence.

Certain items enjoy their own symbolism. Apples, for example, have a role in many ancient myths and legends. In the Bible, the serpent tempted Eve with an apple, the fruit of the tree of life, so it may represent temptation and discord. It is also a symbol of love and fertility, especially if it is a red apple. If you dream about stealing apples it implies trying to steal a love that is not rightfully yours. Traditionally associated with women's breasts in ancient myths and legends, peaches represent paradise, fertility and immortality in Eastern cultures. Watermelons often indicate pregnancy, simply because of their shape. Bananas are phallic symbols, although a banana

skin, something upon which we slip, is a symbol of bad luck. Cherries may feature as a pun: 'life is not a bowl of cherries' implies that things are not going well for the dreamer and in American slang 'losing one's cherry' refers to loss of virginity. Grapes have been grown since ancient times and are a symbol of wealth as well as decadence – one only has to think of Roman nobles being fed grapes by slaves while reclining on their couches. Vines are hardy plants, which entwine themselves around other plants, so they may represent the joy of a close relationship. Aromatic, zesty and bitter, lemons may represent arguments, perhaps because they are not quite the sweet fruit that appearances would have us believe. Lemons are traditionally symbols of fidelity, but if you dream of eating one, it is a sign that disagreements will follow.

Nuts are usually encased within a hard shell and nut dreams may feature a pun such as 'he's a hard nut to crack', or, 'she's nuts about him.' Dreams about cracking nuts imply that the dreamer is

Curvy yellow bananas are associated with fun and slapstick comedy (slipping on a banana skin is often regarded as funny), but they also hint at disappointment.

Bitter lemons may symbolise arguments in dreams.

searching for the truth about something. Orange blossom is traditionally a symbol of fidelity and purity before marriage, but the colour of oranges themselves symbolises extrovert behaviour and an outgoing

Small creatures gather in nuts to hoard them during the winter and so nuts have come to represent prosperity.

Earthy potatoes are a simple, staple food and a dream about them may remind the dreamer to tackle basic issues in his or her life.

lifestyle. Raspberries are hardy, surviving in chilly climates against the odds to produce delicious fruit, so in a dream they can symbolise the rewards of hard work. They may also be a pun: perhaps the dreamer thinks someone is 'blowing raspberries' at him?

Vegetables are connected with the earth and practical values; they take months to grow and nurture, and imply that you should persevere with your work, even if you experience hard times. They are a reminder to concentrate on the essential things in life and to ignore unimportant things. Potatoes, which develop underground, symbolise part of the unconscious mind, although there are several uncomplimentary phrases, such as 'potato head', or 'couch potato' which may also crop up. They are a staple food and obviously associated with the earth, so may imply that the dreamer should apply himself to the elemental things in life, or tackle the roots of his problems. Potatoes may appear in dreams raw or cooked, and they can easily assume faces and shapes, perhaps transforming themselves into monsters. Carrots may be an oblique reference to a red-haired friend; it is probably their colour that has given them the symbolism of treasure and they may refer to buried cash.

Pungent and rotund, cabbages are another vegetable that formed part of a peasant's staple diet for centuries. Savoy and white cabbages are believed to have healing properties, so dreaming about them may symbolise revitalisation. Cucumbers have undoubted phallic symbolism, but, like cabbages, they also denote a recovery from illness. Asparagus is another phallic symbol and in dreams indicates that a passionate relationship is on the horizon.

Mushrooms, which grow in dirt in the dark, imply that a you can expect a small surprise, although since 1945, the phrase 'mushroom cloud' has had more dangerous and sinister connotations that may also feature in dreams. Magic mushrooms have hallucinatory qualities and dream mushrooms may refer to magical happenings.

Cabbage has a poor reputation as an uninteresting vegetable, but herbalists have long acknowledged their healing properties and in dreams they may symbolise restoration.

Mushrooms are famously kept in the dark with mud piled on them, so a dream about mushrooms may reflect similar fears on the part of the dreamer. Mushrooms and toadstools have magical associations in many folk legends.

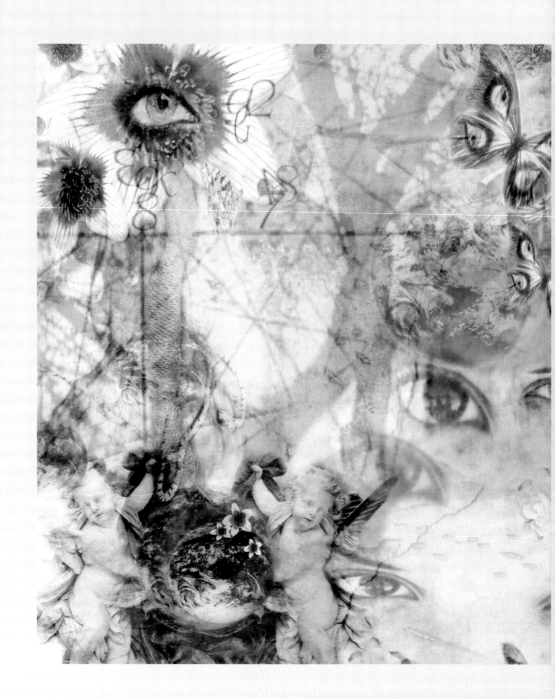

Chapter 7

Animals
- real and unreal

'She felt that she was dozing off, and had just begun to dream that she was walking hand in hand with Dinah, and saying to her very earnestly, 'Now, Dinah, tell me the truth: did you ever eat a bat?'

Lewis Carroll *Alice in Wonderland*

In literature animals have long been used to symbolise aspects of human emotions and traits. People in all cultures have attributed certain anthropomorphic characteristics to particular animals for centuries, and in dreams they often emphasise partially hidden or repressed aspects of our own personalities. Animals may represent urgent, unthinking emotions, animal vitality and energy or at worst, crude, animalistic behaviour. If you dream you are struggling to control an animal, it may be that you are trying to tame the instincts expressed by that particular creature. If an animal threatens you in a dream, try to tame it rather than kill it; if it is slaughtered, the instincts it embodies may be completely lost to you. Dreams about animals may also refer to the signs of the zodiac with which they are associated, or in the Far East, with the Chinese astrological system.

In Native American traditions, wise men or shamans, often assume the form of animals in their dreams – creatures that act as guides during the shaman's journey to other worlds. Mythical beasts, such as unicorns or centaurs may also appear, perhaps created by the subconscious from memories of childhood fairy tales to tackle personal fears. The meanings attributed to dream animals, both real and unreal, lie partly in the dreamer's cultural and personal attitudes to them. Dragons, for example, are generally regarded as fearsome creatures in Western civilisation, whereas in China, they are powerful symbols of good luck. Similarly, dogs are traditionally considered to represent fidelity and loyalty, but a person who has been attacked by a dog is unlikely to view them in the same way in his dreams.

Animals

In dreams animals may express aspects of ourselves or people we know, or may symbolise emotions or fears. Dogs are reputedly faithful and loyal creatures, so a dream about walking a dog may encourage the dreamer to express his loyalty to a cause or person more clearly, for example, while a dream about a lion, the proud king of the jungle, may encourage the dreamer in his ambition to gain promotion at work. The strength and reliability of many domestic animals are generally less threatening than the untamed power of wild creatures, and peaceful animals in dreams may augur success and prosperity, while fighting off a fierce animal represents bravery against overwhelming odds. The appearance of animals in dreams implies that the basest, most instinctive human responses are emerging from under the veneer of civilisation, which separates humankind from beasts.

Dogs are generally regarded as faithful domestic companions, although mythology abounds with more vicious multi-headed beasts such as Cerberus.

'The king of the jungle', lions have a proud demeanour and embody power and pride. They may represent the archetype of the admirable father.

One of the most famous Biblical dreams was Pharaoh's dream about seven healthy cattle and seven lean beasts. A dream about a herd of identical cattle may symbolise the dreamer's desire to part of a crowd.

Domestic creatures – cats, dogs, horses, cows, sheep and pigs – tend to seem more familiar than wild animals and personify less dramatic characteristics. They are beasts of burden or herd animals, and symbolise tamer, less passionate emotions. In Biblical times, a man's wealth was measured by the number of cattle he possessed, and so in dreams fat cattle indicate prosperity, while thinner beasts are symbolic of leaner times. One of the most famous Biblical dreams featured cattle: 'Pharaoh dreamed that he was standing by the Nile, and there came up out of the Nile seven sleek and fat cows and they grazed in the reed grass. Then seven other cows, ugly and thin, came up out of the Nile after them and stood by the other cows on the banks of the Nile. The ugly and thin cows ate up the seven sleek and fat cows. And Pharaoh awoke.' (Gen. 41, vs. 1-4). Pharaoh remained puzzled by his dream for some time, until Joseph was summoned to interpret it. He correctly predicted seven prosperous years would be followed by seven years of hardship, although he attributed his skill to the Almighty. 'It is not I; God will give Pharaoh a favourable answer'. (Gen. 41 vs. 16).

Bulls are particularly powerful animals
with especially masculine associations.
Aggressive and single-minded, bulls
have personified male sexual passion
since Zeus disguised himself as a bull to
woo Europa. Cows, however, are far
more docile, and the term bovine can
have connotations of laziness. Sacred
creatures in the Hindu religion, cows
are maternal figures, and their milk is a
staple of the human diet. Do not
dismiss dream cows: they are solid
creatures, sometimes representing the
mother goddess, who should remind
you of your home, family and roots.
Oxen, castrated bulls, are symbols of
power and patience; they also work
hard and these are the qualities applied
to those born in the Chinese year of the
ox. The second sign of the zodiac,
Taurus the bull, denotes qualities of
practicality, sensuality and, like a typical
bull, anger when thwarted.

Sheep are not renowned for their
cunning or intelligence; they are
animals that live in flocks and rarely
exhibit any initiative in their behaviour.
Ironically, they often appear in the
minds of insomniacs who are advised to
'count sheep' before they sleep! If you
dream you are part of a flock of sheep,

Bulls are powerful masculine symbols, which
sometimes embody aggression and anger. An
angry dreamer may project his suppressed
aggression in this way. Taurus the bull is the
second sign of the zodiac and if it features in your
dreams, you may aspire to the characteristics of
the sign.

you may be concerned that you have lost your individuality or powers of independence. Gentle creatures, lambs are important in Christian symbolism and if you dream of a lamb in distress, it may be indicative of a situation in which you feel like a lamb going to the slaughter; if it has a bloodstained fleece, an innocent person may be suffering as a result of another's error. A dream featuring a healthy flock of sheep reflects a profitable business enterprise; they are especially significant in the dreams of teachers or people who work with 'flocks' of others.

Bleating sheep follow each other around, rarely acting on their own initiative. A dreamer who relishes the role of 'pastoral care' for others may see himself in the position of shepherd. Lambs are reputedly meek and biddable. Cuddly and sweet they are regarded as innocent creatures. Like all young creatures in dreams, they are associated with optimism and new beginnings.

A ram may be part of a pun – perhaps the dreamer feels someone is trying to 'ram something down his throat', and ignoring his opinions.

Those born in the Chinese year of the sheep (or ram) are likewise gentle, compassionate, and sensitive. Rams symbolise powerful friends in dream interpretation. They can be stubborn creatures and if one threatens you in a dream, it may be a sign that your luck is about to run out. The zodiac sign, Aries the ram is characterised by qualities of leadership, aggression and single-mindedness, and a dream ram may in fact refer to a person who was born under this sign.

Goats have traditionally acquired the characteristics of lechery and lust and if a woman dreams about a goat she may fear the advances of a predator.

Goats are renowned for being lusty, and almost scavenging animals that will consume anything. If farmers dream about goats, it is a sign that their crops will flourish, and for others, implies that they will achieve their ambitions. Goats were also a traditional symbol of lechery and a man may be called an 'old goat' if he is in a relationship with a younger woman. Goats work hard to scavenge a living from rough surroundings and those born under the zodiac sign of Capricorn the goat are likewise ambitious, tenacious and loyal. Goats were sometimes used to lure wild beasts into traps, so the dream may refer to a 'scapegoat', one who is an innocent victim.

In medieval times, goats were associated with the Devil possibly because they are such destructive animals.

This image encapsulates 'pork barrel traders', politicians who promote local interests.

Pigs suffer from a mixed reputation, but generally porcine metaphors are unflattering: you may be accused of eating like a pig, behaving like a swine or simply recoil from being called a stupid pig. Pigs are actually clean animals and their reputation for ignorance and poor behaviour is unfair; in Chinese astrology people born in the year of the pig are regarded as honest, good humoured and sensual. Nevertheless, pigs are generally seen to embody the grosser side of human nature, and it is usually this that emerges in dream imagery.

Riding a horse is both liberating and empowering.

Horses have been used by humans as pack animals and a means of transport, and so represent energy or the personal driving force behind the dreamer. Horses are powerful creatures, but can usually be controlled by their human owners, just as we have control over the amount of energy we devote to activities. Dreams about riding may indicate liberation as the dreamer flees from everyday responsibilities. Those born in the year of the horse are reputed to be fickle, optimistic and determined. The colour of the dream horse may be significant: white horses, which feature frequently in myths and legends, are usually symbols of renewal and optimism, while black horses signify bad news. Donkeys are said to be a sign of poor decisions that may later rebound on the dreamer.

Donkeys have a reputation as gloomy animals.

Beasts of burden and 'ships of the desert', dream camels may indicate that you are long-suffering and carrying too much responsibility. Elephants are considered to be wonderful symbols of good luck and prosperity in dreams, particularly if you have a dream about feeding an elephant. Their great bulk represents the dreamer's financial position, so feeding the animal is symbolic of investing in your future.

Camels represent burdens and responsibility.

Haughty and aloof, cats are often associated with witches and may have magical connotations. A dream cat may appear as some sort of 'familiar' friend guiding the dreamer through the story.

Dogs and cats often appear as talking companions in dreams, possibly because as household pets, they seem to be familiar friends.

'Man's best friend', dogs often denote protection, friendships and faithfulness (all qualities applied to those born in the year of the dog), although try to remember whether the dream dog appeared friendly or vicious. A vicious dog may hint that a friend will turn against you. Dogs may appear in dreams as guides and, traditionally, dogs are guardians of the underworld. Cats are less biddable creatures, their feline eccentricities often appearing more intuitive and feminine. Aloof creatures of the night, they are sometimes associated with witches and magic, especially black cats, although they are also symbols of good luck in Britain. Ancient dream analysts believed that dreaming of a cat meant that you were about to be robbed or that a friend would become treacherous. Cats may seem mercurial, so if one appears in your dreams watch its movements and demeanour carefully; a dirty cat may be a sign of bad luck, whereas a cat that is washing itself is a sign of good fortune.

Fecund and numerous, rabbits are most obviously associated with fertility,
but cuddly toy rabbits also have strong associations with childhood.

Rabbits are often cited as symbols of fertility and a rabbit's paw is a traditional sign of good luck. Chinese astrology believes that the year of the rabbit endows people with sensitivity, harmony and good fortune. Dream rabbits denote happiness in your relationships and are an auspicious symbol in the dreams of those who want to have children. Hares have slightly different symbolism and a dream of a hare racing away from you may imply that a house move is on the horizon.

Wild animals are the embodiment of power, freedom and untamed instincts. Their appearance in our dreams may be simple wish fulfilment; the dreamer may long to cast off the restrictive behaviour imposed by his domestic routine and embrace the freedom of the wild. Alternatively, wild animals may stand for danger, the sheer strength of the creatures threatening to overturn settled existences. Lions present an image of grandeur, dignity, courage and danger; they are watchful and poised to chase prey. They are masculine figures, often symbols of leadership and, in several cultures, personify the sun. Tigers are also powerful felines, although they have come to denote stealth and cruelty; in dreams they stand for the threats posed by a hidden danger. In China, however, tigers are an expression of royalty and courage, the qualities apparently personified by those born in the year of the tiger.

Proud, fearless and deadly, tigers are beautiful yet threatening dream visitors. 'Paper tigers', however, are animals or people which appear strong, but actually pose no threat at all.

Lumbering, enormous elephants proverbially 'never forget' and in the East are associated with royalty. A dream about riding an elephant suggests a desire to rise above others and ride around in a stately fashion. A dream about feeding an elephant augurs well for your prosperity, but if you dream that an elephant is trampling everything around it, your finances are out of control.

Elephants are regarded as wise animals, and famously 'never forget'. These attributes may in part stem from Hindu mythology, in which Ganesh, the elephant-headed son of Shiva is regarded as the god of wisdom.

Dreams about rhinos are probably reasonably rare unless you are a zookeeper or live in the African bush, but should one appear, it presages an increasingly exciting sex life – powdered rhino horn has long been upheld as an aphrodisiac.

Rhinos are robust animals, and insensitive people are often credited with having a rhino's skin. In dream symbolism, rhinos may also represent sexual urges.

Dream bears often resemble those in fairy tales and may represent an aspect of the dreamer's character or someone close to them.

Bears appear as friendly, if sometimes, gruff beasts in children's fairy tales, yet real bears are bad-tempered and often violent animals, as far removed as possible from the cuddly teddies of childhood. Their sheer power and strength are important factors and some cultures, particularly the Lapps, hold them in great respect. They are often used to symbolise military leadership, while a female bear represents the mother who 'bears' children. A dream bear symbolises elemental power and the capricious, random force of nature that drives them and, indeed, the negative side of the dreamer's character (his 'shadow').

Monkeys are the creatures which most resemble humans and are traditionally regarded as mischievous and intelligent. In Chinese astrology the year of the monkey endows these qualities, along with versatility and humour. Monkeys emphasise the childlike part of us and in dreams may refer to arrested development or even a desire to regress to the behaviour of our ancestral primates. They may also signify the trickster and appear this way in both Native American and Hindu mythology.

Monkeys are regarded as playful rogues in Chinese Buddhist legend an impetuous magical monkey plays an important role. If you are faced with a monkey in your dreams, treat it with caution.

Wolves are animals that share a long-standing relationship with mankind and in mythology are generally creatures that inspire fear and loathing or sometimes, sneaking admiration. Dreaming of a wolf may be a sign that someone is about to take advantage of you, perhaps someone you regard as a friend, or a 'wolf in sheep's clothing'. Wolves are predatory creatures, wild animals that threaten animals and sometimes poorly defended people. They feature in fairy tales, sometimes disguising themselves to take advantage of the weak, and may appear in dreams in this guise. An

Wolves enjoy a mixed reputation, on one hand regarded as admirable, noble creatures, on the other as predatory, vicious beasts.

alternative view is that wolves are noble, wild beasts, which live free from restraint, so if your dream wolf elicits envy, perhaps you need to roam free from the confines of your everyday life for a while. Native American tradition holds the wolf as a sacred animal – a guide and the fount of ancient wisdom.

The 'wolf in sheep's clothing' metaphor sums up the dangers of trusting someone's outer appearance. A dream of this nature may imply that someone is trying to take advantage of the dreamer.

Stags, 'the monarchs of the glen' are strong masculine symbols with clear sexual imagery.

With their monumental antlers, stags are proud, powerful masculine creatures that represent masculine sexual power in dreams. They dominate herds of graceful female deer and as such are the source of metaphors relating to bachelors: grooms enjoy an all-male stag party on the eve of their wedding, and a man with several girlfriends may be referred to as a bit of a stag.

Rats and other small rodents enjoy mixed symbolism. Mice are traditionally shy creatures, their tiny size ensuring that they can scurry around virtually unseen. Many people are scared of mice and they may be an indication of small problems that the dreamer has got out of proportion. Rats and other

Almost universally reviled, a plague of rats may appear in a nightmare. In Chinese astrology the rat is attributed with the qualities of affirmative action, expansion and wealth.

rodents usually elicit stronger responses, as they carry disease. Associated with treachery, dream rats may indicate that a friend is working against you or that someone is taking advantage of you; they may feature in dreams warning that you should beware of tangling with unscrupulous persons. If you dream about killing a rat, it stands for your ability to successfully defend yourself against these threats. By contrast, the Chinese year of the rat promises wealth, expansion and positive action.

Moles are subterranean animals that dig up molehills where they are least wanted. A dream about a mole may indicate that someone is undermining your position at work.

Moles probably feature in dreams as a pun, perhaps suggesting that the dreamer is struggling too much with a problem and 'making a mountain out of a molehill'.

Birds and insects

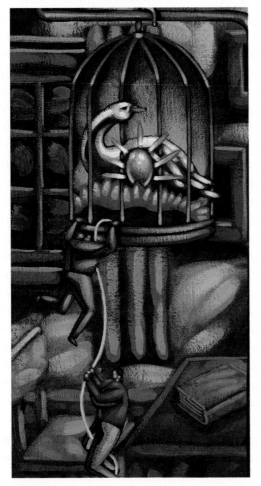

A caged bird is a poor imprisoned creature and in dreams may represent the dreamer's hopes which are imprisoned by stronger influences.

Birds symbolise freedom, as their flight is not constrained by boundaries or borders.

Birds are masters of the skies and connect earthly beings with the heavens. They represent freedom and the ability to fly high and look at the earth from a different perspective. Dream birds may help the dreamer connect with a higher spiritual plane or point to the way forward in the achievement of ambitions; they often appear in dreams as messengers. High-flying birds are particularly auspicious and point to successful schemes, but caged birds suggest that the dreamer's aspirations are restricted or trapped. A flock of birds (particularly black ones) may represent the legal profession; the sound of bird song hints at celebrations or weddings, although blackbirds, magpies and crows suggest funerals and, together with ravens, are traditionally believed to herald death. A dream about caged birds means that part of the dreamer's hopes or ambitions are restricted for some reason and the dreamer wants to free them in order to roam free in the skies of his or her intellect. A dream about a

A flock of birds is a glorious sight, although they can appear intimidating. Alfred Hitchcock's memorable 1963 film *The Birds* successfully explored the threatening nature of these innocent creatures.

With glossy black feathers, ravens appear as harbingers of doom. At the Tower of London, they have acquired a protective mythology of their own as legend suggests that the tower will fall if the ravens leave.

multi-coloured flock of birds is a sign of an optimistic, joyful soul who is embracing the challenges of the future.

Forbidding and black, ravens represented the devil in traditional folklore and in dreams may also personify the 'shadow', the dark side of a dreamer's personality. Doves are the opposite of this image, and stand for peace and happiness in love, as well as freedom and simplicity.

Beautiful, graceful and slightly enigmatic, swans feature in both Celtic and Greek mythology. Fionnuala, daughter of Lir was transformed into a swan and condemned to wander Ireland for many hundreds of years.

Swallows are often the first sign of the arrival of spring. Although 'one swallow does not summer make', they are symbols of optimism and faithfulness, as they return to nest in the same place year after year. They may appear as a pun, possibly reminding the dreamer that he has to 'swallow his pride'.

Majestic, forbidding birds, eagles and hawks are sacred birds in many cultures. With the ability to fly high and look directly at the sun, they are often regarded as messengers from the gods. In dreams they may stand for ambition and dominance. Owls are often associated with wisdom as they sit inscrutably in trees waiting for the right moment to pounce on their prey. As they work mainly in the dark they are also associated with the souls of the dead, but in dreams they are more usually linked with guidance.

Magnificent and imposing, eagles are a patriotic symbol of the USA and are sacred birds in Native American legend.

Ducks might feature as a pun in dreams: perhaps the dreamer is 'ducking' his responsibilities, or should 'duck out' of a tricky relationship or situation. Perhaps the dreamer is feeling like a 'sitting duck'.

Ducks represent a bright future for the dreamer and his or her family. Ugly ducklings proverbially turn into swans, graceful and dignified creatures whose appearance in a dream indicates an improvement in financial or business affairs. More traditionally, swans symbolise the Mother Goddess and may appear as a farewell symbol, as in 'swan song'. Chickens and hens warn against selfishness, while cocks crowing in the morning may indicate an early marriage and a luxurious life. Cockerels are traditional symbols of lust and a dream of cocks crowing in the evening, traditionally a sign of bad luck, signifies a late marriage and years of poverty. Cockfights warn of family quarrels, while hens may herald a family reunion. Those born in the year of the rooster are characterised by fairness and loyalty.

Fragile and striking, butterflies are the product of a remarkable transformation and so symbolise change.

Symbols of progress, butterflies signify prosperity, success and change – they are, after all, creatures that are the product of a remarkable metamorphosis. Ants are insects renowned for their hard work and in dreams represent satisfaction with a job well done. Bees are also regarded as industrious creatures and in dreams indicate success, progress and wealth as a result of relentless labour. Traditional dream interpretation states that a dream about a swarm of bees is a warning to guard against fire erupting in the home. Conversely, small beetles and bugs that scurry around the edges of the dream world warn of small setbacks or losses.

Spiders, which are feared by many people, are important symbols in Indian symbolism because their web replicates the rays of the sun. In some African societies, spiders play an important part in creation myths and it is believed that they spun the stuff that humans are made of. For many Western dreamers, however, the negative imagery associated with spiders, which spin a web to entrap creatures, will be uppermost in their dreams. A dream about spinning a web is a symbol of good fortune: it represents the power of the dreamer to protect himself with a web of his own creation and to control events around him.

Arachnophobes are likely to have nightmares about spiders, but they are hard-working creatures and may symbolise honest toil. Depending on your viewpoint, spiders' webs are either ingenious means of acquiring food, or malicious deathtraps.

Fish, serpents and amphibians

A dream about fish swimming in the sea implies that the dreamer has an inquiring outlook on the world.

In dream imagery, anything to do with water represents the unconscious or emotions, so fish, the primitive ancestors of humans, are symbolic of elusive emotions, possibly those from the past, struggling to surface. Dreaming of seas or waterways thriving with colourful fish is a sign of a healthy emotional life, with plenty of friends and contacts. Dreams of dead fish, however, signify a more troubled soul: perhaps the dreamer is unhappy and feels deserted by those he cares for. If you dream of fish swimming against a current, it denotes some sort of conflict in your emotional life, one that must be addressed by recognising the issues and bringing them to the surface of your conscious mind. A dream about eating fish represents rebirth or reawakening, as fish (in Christian belief) is a miraculous food.

Traditional interpreters believe that a dream about eating fish means that the dreamer will form warm and lasting attachments with new acquaintances.

Salmon are sacred symbols of knowledge in Celtic and North American traditions, and eating them apparently conferred infinite wisdom. The life cycle of salmon, which return to the same breeding ground year on year after travelling great distances, implies impressive inherited genetic memory.

Aquatic mammals, such as dolphins, are creatures of prodigious intelligence and embody wisdom and understanding. Many people who swim with dolphins report that they are profoundly moved by the experience and a dolphin may carry an important message in dreams, representing the fusion of air and water, or the conscious and the subconscious. The symbolism of dolphins is completely positive, as they are a sign of friendship, guidance, intelligence and enlightenment.

Dolphins are often credited with intelligence on a par with that of humans and may feature in 'great dreams' which provide guidance and advice.

Amphibians seem slimy and thus have implications of distrust. Frogs acquire magical qualities in fairy tales, their slimy outer appearance often hiding a gorgeously rich prince. And so in dreams, do not dismiss frogs as squat green amphibians, but try to see if they have hidden depths or are hiding something. They are creatures of transition (because of their transformation from tadpoles to frogs) and a dream frog may lead you to a surprising place. Toads are physically similar to frogs, but somehow lack their magical charm and are associated with ugliness and stubbornness. They often denote problems and losses, but if the toad hops away, this suggests that you will overcome them.

One creature with strong associations of evil, certainly in Christian symbolism, is the serpent or snake. With a reputation for malevolence stretching right back to Adam and Eve in the Garden of Eden, snakes have something of an image problem. They have personified wicked deeds, duplicity and entrapment for centuries, so if one approaches in your dreams, treat it with care. They may also be phallic symbols and, generally, snake

Slimy, squat frogs may hide their true selves; look around your dream frog to see whether there are clues to their true purpose.

Slippery and dangerous, snakes are regarded as untrustworthy. Is there a snake in the grass of your dream?

245

Long-lived tortoises stand for slow but steady progress and reliability.

Crocodiles warn dreamers to beware of false friends, who may shed 'crocodile tears'.

dreams occur when a dreamer is feeling sexually repressed. Snakes also embody wisdom, however, and are the symbol of Western medicine. Their symbolism is both contradictory and fascinating and they are an important archetype.

Tortoises are the complete opposite and usually symbolise long life and slow but steady progress; they can represent perseverance and endurance, too. Crocodiles and alligators appear frequently in dreams, representatives of the darkest depths of the unconscious mind. Rather like the snake, they inherit two different areas of symbolism. An antediluvian creature, it may signify ancestral wisdom, and in some cultures is endowed with qualities of enlightenment. However, it is also a brutally fast killer, which lurks unseen in rivers and lakes, and so it may be regarded as the arbiter of life and death.

Shellfish or crustaceans such as lobsters and crabs have admirable protective armour, but they are primitive life forms which represent partly formed ideas and energies. Their hard exterior contrasts with a tender interior, so they signify an unwillingness to open up emotionally. Furthermore, crabs are known for scuttling sideways and symbolise an inability to confront a problem head-on. Some Freudian analysts believe that the shapes of shells and shellfish resemble the female genitalia, so a man who dreams of admiring or collecting shells may be expressing a hidden sexual urge. Crabs may also be a reference to those born under the sign of Cancer, traditionally loyal, sensitive and tenacious souls. Scorpions are more predatory and dangerous creatures and symbolise the danger posed by treacherous friends; if you kill one in your dreams, you may well overcome your enemies. Alternatively, dream scorpions may represent those born under the zodiac sign of Scorpio, probably an energetic and sociable individual.

Crustaceans are reminiscent of primitive life forms. More pertinently, they are protected by their shell and in dreams may serve to remind the dreamer that he needs to cultivate a tougher outer armour.

The appearance of Cancer the crab may reflect a dreamer's fears about his health or that of someone close.

Mythical beasts

Unspeakable monsters often personify children's fears in their dreams as children are sometimes less able to articulate their uncertainties.

Mythical creatures such as phoenixes, griffins, dragons or unicorns may appear in really memorable or transforming dreams and their presence is often regarded with awe by dream interpreters. Although mythical creatures are the products of the human imagination and have been created to cope with unspeakable fears, they are significant factors in the dream world.

They sometimes crop up in what Jung referred to as 'big' dreams, those which leave the dreamer feeling changed and revitalised, having experienced an intense dream that has especially strong significance for their life. Such dreams may deal with the great fundamentals of human existence and as such feature archetypes, astonishing landscapes, unearthly music and strange creatures. These dreams may be based on great myths, stories or even films, with witches, wizards, fairies,

ogres and other enchanted creatures in the dream cast. They are likely to be rooted in childhood stories and the recurrence of these creatures may indicate a refusal to face unnamed terrors in waking life; the dreamer is taking refuge in his childhood to protect himself.

In western legends, fire-breathing dragons often protect a secret of some sort of treasure. A dream dragon may represent a similar sort of custodial role.

Dragons are regarded with fear in Western civilizations – as fire-breathing monsters that are out to grill noble princes and heroes. Jung believed that they were important symbols, representing the evil side of the Great Mother archetype, but in China they are seen as a sign of good luck. If you are faced with a dragon in your dreams,

confront it and try to see what it is hiding or guarding; it may be necessary to slay the dragon in order to progress. The dragon is the foremost animal of the Chinese zodiac, bestowing energy and enthusiasm on those born under its sign.

Beautiful and rare even in mythology, unicorns are symbols of purity, although their horns may be seen as phallic symbols. Unicorns can be both aggressive and gentle and they appear opposite the lion in heraldry. The phoenix, a creature that rises up from the ashes of its own immolation, is a symbol of rebirth. If a phoenix appears in your dreams, consider whether there is an aspect of your life or career that could be burnt and transformed into something new and fresh. These creatures are an expression of optimism and hope in the future.

Phoenixes signify great hope and optimism, and are symbols of rebirth.

Centaurs are half man and half horse, creatures with the intellectual capacity of a man and the speed and strength of a horse; in mythology they are often mercurial and untrustworthy, although they have powers of protection, too. People born under the sign of Sagittarius the archer are said to possess the impetuosity of horses and the creative brilliance of humans. Mermaids also mix human and animal characteristics, where the cold intellect of humans combines with the sensitive emotional symbolism associated with water. In legends, mermaids lured sailors to a watery grave and even if the mermaid herself does not seem alluring, the presence of water suggests that the dream is concerned with emotional undercurrents.

Centaurs embody the characteristics of man and horse. In mythology they are sometimes regarded as unreliable, even threatening creatures.

Talking animals may also appear in your dreams and are probably reminiscent of half-remembered fairy tales from childhood. They are often wise creatures, proffering advice or guidance.

Beautiful mermaids were once believed to lure innocent sailors to their deaths, so if a mermaid appears in your dream, approach it with caution.

Epilogue

Reputable dream analysts all stress that dream dictionaries cannot offer hard and fast interpretations of the symbols and images in everybody's dreams. They can, however, make suggestions and educate dreamers in the traditional associations of some common symbols and types of dream. The personal circumstances of the dreamer are just as important as the images the dreamer recounts. In short, apply the context of your life, activities and memories to dream images and you will be well on the way towards making sense of your dreams and increasing your self-knowledge.

In 1816 the romantic poet George Gordon, Lord Byron, a man infamous for his unorthodox lifestyle and probably plagued by dreams which attempted to make sense of it, summed up the effect of dreams on our lives more elegantly than any other writer in his poem *The Dream*.

'Our life is twofold; Sleep hath its own world,
A boundary between the things misnamed
Death and existence: Sleep hath its own world,
And a wide realm of wild reality,
And dreams in their development have breath,
And tears, and tortures, and the touch of joy;
They leave a weight upon our waking thoughts,
They take a weight from off waking toils,
They do divide our being; they become
A portion of ourselves as of our time,
And look like heralds of eternity;
They pass like spirits of the past—they speak
Like sibyls of the future; they have power—
The tyranny of pleasure and of pain;
They make us what we were not—what they will,
And shake us with the vision that's gone by,
The dread of vanished shadows—Are they so?
Is not the past all shadow?—What are they?
Creations of the mind?—The mind can make
Substances, and people planets of its own
With beings brighter than have been, and give
A breath to forms which can outlive all flesh.
I would recall a vision which I dreamed
Perchance in sleep—for in itself a thought,
A slumbering thought, is capable of years,
And curdles a long life into one hour.'

Bibliography

Barrett, David V., *Dreams*, Dorling Kindersley, 1995
Chetwynd, Tom, *Dictionary for Dreamers*, Thorsons, 1972
Daco, Pierre, *Interpret Your Dreams*, Robinson Books, 1993
Dee, Nerys, *Understanding dreams*, Thorsons, 1991
Fenton, Sasha *An illustrated guide to dream meaning*, D&S Books, 2001
Fontana, David, *The Secret Language of Dreams*, Pavilion Books, 1994
Francis, Val, *Illustrated Guide to Dreams*, Bison Books, 1995
Gibson, Clare, *The Ultimate Birthday Book*, Saraband, 1998
Holloway, Gillian, *Dream Discoveries Newsletter*, website: www.lifetreks.com/lifetreks3/article04.asp
Innes, Brian, *The Book of Dreams*, Brown Packaging Books, 2000
Jung, Carl, *Man and his Symbols*, Arkana, 1990
Miller, Gustavus Hindman, *The Wordsworth Dictionary of Dreams*, Wordsworth Editions, 1994
Millidge Judith, *Dream Symbols*, Saraband, 1998
Morgan Lucien, *Dreams and Symbols*, Tiger Books, 1996
Parker, Julia & Derek, *The Complete Book of Dreams*, Dorling Kindersley, 1995,
Peters, Dr. Roderick, *Living with Dreams*, Andre Deutsch, 1990
Simmons, Michele & McLaughlin, Chris, *Dream Interpretation for Beginners*, Headway, 1994

Credits & acknowledgements

I am very grateful to the many friends and members of my family who shared their dreams with me… and chortled with incredulity as I attempted to tell them what it all meant.

This is dedicated to my family: Jonathan, my sleeping partner; and Lizzie and Jake, the disturbers of my sleep and focus of my dreams.

Picture Credits

Images pp 6, 7t, 8, 11b, 12, 15-16, 18-23, 28, 29t, 30, 33, 35, 37, 38t, 41, 44, 46, 52b, 53-57, 59-60, 62-64, 65b, 67bl & br, 69, 70t, 72t, 74m, 75, 76t & m, 77b, 78, 79r, 80t, 81t, 82b, 83-84, 85b, 86, 87l, 88, 91l, 92, 94, 97l, 98b, 99, 100t, 101t, 102t, 103b, 104t, 105b, 106-108, 110b, 111-112, 114t, 115-116, 121r, 123, 124t, 125b, 126, 127l, 129b, 132r, 133, 134, 140b, 141, 142, 143t, 144b, 145t, 146b, 147b, 149b, 150t, 151, 152-153, 156-160, 161t, 163b, 164t, 165-166, 169, 171t, 172, 173t, 174-177, 179b, 181, 182l, 183, 189-190, 192, 193b, 194, 196b, 197, 198t, 199, 200t, 201b, 202b, 203t, 204b, 205, 207-212, 214-220, 224t, 225, 226b, 227, 228t, 229b, 231-237, 238l, 241-242, 244b, 245-250 © Getty Images

Images pp 7b, 10, 11t, 13-14, 26b, 27, 32, 34, 36, 38b, 39-40, 42-43, 48-51, 52t, 58, 65t, 67bl & tr, 68, 70-71, 72b, 73, 74t & b, 76b, 77t, 79l & m, 80b, 81b, 82t, 85t, 87r, 89l, 90, 96, 97r, 98t, 100b, 101b, 102b, 103t, 104b, 105t, 109, 110b, 113, 114b, 118-120, 121l, 122, 124b, 125t, 127t & m, 128, 129t, 130, 131b, 132l, 136-139, 140t, 143b, 144t, 145b, 146t, 147t, 148, 149t, 150b, 154, 161b, 162, 163t, 164b, 170, 171b, 173b, 179t, 180, 182r, 184-188, 193t, 194, 196t, 198b, 200b, 201t, 202t, 203b, 204t, 206, 213, 223, 224b, 226t, 238r, 239-240, 243, © Stockbyte

Images pp25, 26t © Corbis

Illustrations pp17, 24, 91r by Chloe Leaper.   Illustration p131t by Peter Mallison

Images p89b, 228b, 229t, 230 by Paul Forrester   Images p116, 244t by Colin Bowling.